DISCOVERIES IN SPACE SCIENCE

The Solar System

GENERAL EDITORS:
Giles Sparrow, Judith John, and Chris McNab

Cavendish
Square

New York

Published in 2016 by Cavendish Square Publishing, LLC
243 5th Avenue, Suite 136, New York, NY 10016

First Edition

Website: cavendishsq.com

This publication represents the opinions and views of the author based on his or her personal experience, knowledge, and research. The information in this book serves as a general guide only. The author and publisher have used their best efforts in preparing this book and disclaim liability rising directly or indirectly from the use and application of this book.

CPSIA Compliance Information: Batch #CW16CSQ

All websites were available and accurate when this book was sent to press.

Cataloging-in-Publication Data

Sparrow, Giles.
The solar system / edited by Giles Sparrow, Judith John, and Chris McNab.
p. cm. — (Discoveries in space science)
Includes index.
ISBN 978-1-5026-1018-8 (hardcover) ISBN 978-1-5026-1019-5 (ebook)
1. Solar system — Juvenile literature. I. Sparrow, Giles, 1970-. II. John, Judith. III. McNab, Chris, 1970-. IV. Title.
QB501.3 S63 2016
523.2—d23

Project Editor: Michael Spilling
Design: Hawes Design and Mark Batley
Picture Research: Terry Forshaw
Additional Text: Chris McNab and Judith John

All images are taken from the card set Secrets of the Universe (six volumes) published by International Masters Publishers AB, except the following: Chaikovskiy Igor/Shutterstock.com, cover, 1; Flashinmirror/Shutterstock.com, 4–5.

Printed in the United States of America

TABLE OF CONTENTS

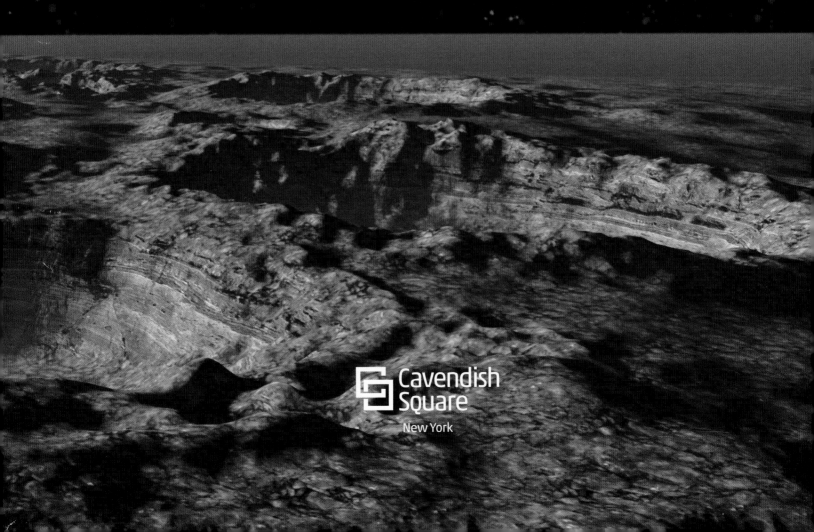

DISCOVERIES IN
SPACE SCIENCE

The Solar System

Cavendish
Square
New York

INTRODUCING THE SOLAR SYSTEM

The solar system consists of everything that comes within the Sun's region of influence—a volume of space extending out to approximately one light-year from the Sun itself. One light-year is about 6 trillion miles (10 trillion kilometers) long. The vast majority of the solar system's material lies much closer to the Sun, however—even Pluto orbits just a few thousand million miles away from the center. This inner region is the realm of the planets, eight of which follow more-or-less circular orbits around the Sun, with the ninth, Pluto—designated a dwarf planet since 2006—in a more elongated orbit. In fact Pluto's original designation as a planet was little more than an accident of history, as we shall see. The major planets divide neatly into two types: rocky or terrestrial planets orbiting close to the Sun (of which Earth is the largest), and giant gas planets such as Jupiter, orbiting farther out. Many of the planets have their own natural satellites or moons, and the gas giants are also encircled by ring systems, of which Saturn's is the most spectacular. A belt of rocky asteroids divides the terrestrials from the giants between Mars and Jupiter, while beginning around Neptune's orbit is the Kuiper Belt, a region of small icy worlds of which Pluto is the largest known member. Some comets originate here, while others orbit further out, at the very limits of the Sun's gravitational reach, in the Oort Cloud.

A montage of images shows the planets and four of Jupiter's moons, with the surface of Earth's moon in the foreground.

OVERVIEW OF THE SOLAR SYSTEM

Once, the solar system seemed a simple place, its members forming a neat hierarchy: a central star, nine planets in stately orbit, a dozen or so dead moons, the occasional comet, and a collection of asteroids. At the orbit of Pluto, the most distant dwarf planet, our system appeared to end. In the last 30 years, modern technology has helped to change this simple image. Moons can be larger than planets, and comets swarm by the trillion halfway to the nearest star. We live in a dynamic and complex neighborhood.

SOLAR SYSTEM PROFILE

LIFE-SCALE	4.6 BILLION YEARS
DIAMETER	3 LIGHT-YEARS
DIAMETER OF PLANETARY ZONE	7.4 BILLION MILES (11.9 BILLION KM)
KNOWN PLANETS	9 COMMONLY ACCEPTED
SATELLITES	AT LEAST 140
KNOWN LIFE-BEARING PLANETS	1
LARGEST PLANET	JUPITER (318 TIMES THE MASS OF THE EARTH)
SMALLEST (DWARF) PLANET	PLUTO (ONE-THIRD THE DIAMETER OF THE EARTH)
PLANET WITH FASTEST SPIN	JUPITER (9 HOURS 55.5 MINUTES)

SYSTEM TOUR

As we approach the solar system, the first thing that strikes us is that it is a single-star system. The galaxy is full of multiple star systems, which can lead to very eccentric planet orbits. The Sun's single state may result from its birth in a modest-size gas cloud, leaving it to develop a system of planets that all orbit in the same direction and in the same plane.

This is not to say that everything in the solar system is well organized. In the Oort Cloud, the outermost shell of the solar system, icy bodies orbit slowly in all directions, taking millions of years to do so. But as we move inward, the orbits become more regular. At the fringe of the planetary area lies the Kuiper Belt, home to numerous small ice worlds, including Pluto—

reclassified in 2006 as a dwarf planet—and perhaps several other Kuiper Belt Objects of similar size.

Closer in lie the giant planets, with extended gaseous or liquid atmospheres. The largest, Jupiter, dominates the rest. No planet can exist without feeling the pull of Jupiter, which carries with it most of the solar system's momentum around the Sun.

Closest in are the rocky planets, no more than a tenth the diameter of Jupiter. At their outer fringes are the asteroids, small bodies that were prevented from clumping into a planet by Jupiter's gravity. One of the rocky planets, Earth, has the good fortune to be in an almost circular orbit at a distance from the Sun where water can exist as a liquid on its surface. This has led to a remarkable development—life.

ONE MORE—OR LESS?

IN 2005, ASTRONOMERS ANNOUNCED THE DISCOVERY OF THE FIRST NEW KUIPER BELT OBJECT TO RIVAL PLUTO IN SIZE. THIS WORLD, NICKNAMED "SANTA" FOR ITS DISCOVERY AT CHRISTMAS 2004, ORBITS TWO AND A HALF TIMES FURTHER FROM THE SUN THAN PLUTO. THE DISCOVERY REIGNITED THE DEBATE ABOUT THE NUMBER OF PLANETS—SOME SAID THE NEW OBJECT SHOULD BE CLASSED AS A TENTH PLANET, WHILE OTHERS ARGUED THAT BOTH PLUTO AND SANTA SHOULD BE CLASSED AS DWARF PLANETS. THE LATTER GROUP WERE SUCCESSFUL. IT IS NOW KNOWN OFFICIALLY AS HAUMEA.

JOURNEY TO THE CENTER

The solar system is shrouded in the Oort Cloud. Deep inside this chilly region, the planets orbit the system's central star.

Oort Cloud

Outer Planets

Sun

Jupiter

Saturn

Uranus

Neptune

Pluto

Terrestrial Planets

Mercury

Venus

Earth

Mars

THE HALO
In the Oort Cloud, trillions of comets slowly swarm around the solar system (left). At this immense distance from the Sun—at least one light-year or more—the comets are inert icy cores with chaotic orbits. They only become active—and visible from Earth—when collisions or gravitational encounters drive them toward the inner system.

OUTER PLANETS
Two of the nine planets vie for the distinction of being the most distant from the Sun, Neptune and Pluto. Pluto (left) is a dwarf planet in an elongated orbit that sometimes brings it inside the orbit of Neptune. Even though its has a moon, Charon, Pluto was reclassified as a dwarf planet in 2006.

HEARTLAND
The inner solar system is the home of the rocky planets, Mars, Earth, Venus, and finally Mercury. Earth and Mars (left) orbit within the so-called "life zone"—in which liquid water might exist. On Mars, though, atmospheric conditions make liquid water impossible. So far, life is known to have evolved only on Earth.

PLANETARY ORBITS

The movements of the planets in the sky are not easy to account for. Some follow fairly predictable paths; others roam without any obvious pattern and appear to change direction almost at random. Over the centuries, many of humanity's best brains tried to find an explanation. But until the seventeenth century and the genius of Johannes Kepler, they failed. Kepler was the first to realize that the planetary orbits are ellipses, not circles, and that the Earth moves around the Sun in just the same way as the other planets do.

ORBITS OF THE PLANETS

Planet	Closest to Sun (millions of miles/km)	Farthest from Sun (millions of miles/km)	Orbital Velocity (miles/km per second)	Time Taken for One Orbit
Mercury	28.5/45.9	43.3/69.7	29.80/47.96	87.97 days
Venus	66.7/107.3	67.7/109.0	21.77/35.04	224.70 days
Earth	91.3/146.9	94.4/151.9	18.50/29.77	365.26 days
Mars	129.0/207.6	155.0/249.4	15.00/24.14	686.98 days
Jupiter	460.4/740.9	506.9/815.8	8.11/13.05	11.86 years
Saturn	837.0/1,347.0	936.0/1,506.3	6.00/9.66	29.46 years
Uranus	1,699.0/2,734.3	1,867.0/3,004.6	4.23/6.81	84.07 years
Neptune	2,769.0/4,456.3	2,819.0/4,536.7	3.37/5.42	164.82 years
Pluto	2,939.0/4,729.9	4,583.0/7,375.6	2.90/4.67	248.60 years

CIRCLING THE SUN

When Polish astronomer Nicolas Copernicus died in 1543, he left an explosive legacy to his fellow scholars. In a book that he had quietly prepared for publication after his death, he declared that the Earth was not at the center of the universe, as most scholars and the Church still firmly believed. Instead, the Earth orbited the Sun—just like all the other planets.

But Copernicus was unable to explain just how the planets revolved around the Sun. He believed that they moved in perfect circles or, sometimes, in circles within circles. But observations of the night sky did not match his theory. The main problem was Mars, which seemed to wander back and forth almost as it pleased. Why did Mars move in this way? It was another half

century before the German astronomer Johannes Kepler (1551–1630) provided the answer.

Kepler broadly agreed with Copernicus's theory, but saw the need for fine-tuning, and went to work with Danish astronomer Tycho Brahe (1546–1601). Over the course of several decades, Brahe and his team had logged a huge number of very accurate measurements of Mars's position in the sky. Given Brahe's data—obtained without telescopes—Kepler soon realized that Mars could not orbit the Sun in a perfect circle. By trial and error, he calculated that its course could only be explained if it moved in an ellipse, a type of elongated circle. All points on a circle are the same distance from the center, but an ellipse has two "centers," or foci. And from any point on an ellipse, the sum of the distances to each of the foci remains constant.

KEPLER'S LAWS

If one planet orbited in an ellipse, why not all the others? On that assumption, backed up by careful observation, Kepler proposed three laws of planetary motion. First, planetary orbits are ellipses, with the Sun at one of the foci. Second, a line drawn from the Sun to a moving planet sweeps through equal areas in equal times.

Third, the square of the time each planet takes to orbit the Sun is proportional to the cube of its mean distance from the Sun. The second and third laws mean that a planet moves fastest when it is

closest to the Sun, and slowest when it is most distant. Kepler had discovered that the governing force was gravity. After his death, another great scientist—Isaac Newton (1643–1727)—would explain gravity. But Kepler's laws still hold true, and combined with Newton's laws, they explain the movements of any object in space—planet, satellite, or spacecraft.

Dominating the sky, a rogue planet the size of Jupiter looms above a flooded, stormy Earth. Its gravity would produce tides at least 100 times higher than those raised by the Moon. It would also buckle the Earth's crust and drag our planet into a new orbit.

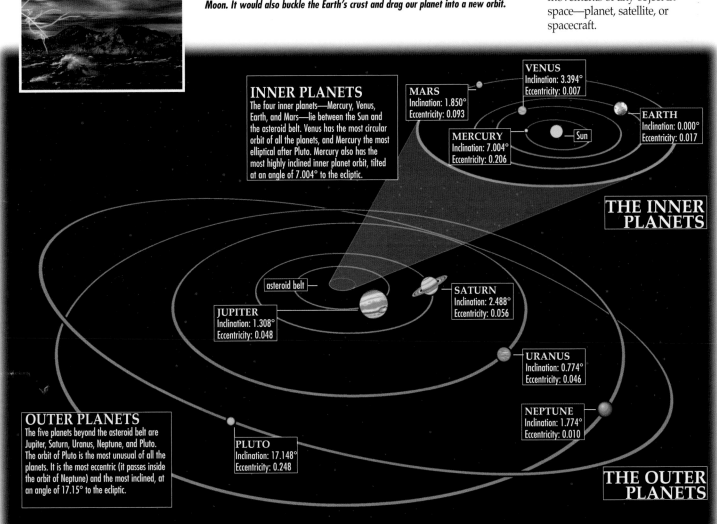

INNER PLANETS
The four inner planets—Mercury, Venus, Earth, and Mars—lie between the Sun and the asteroid belt. Venus has the most circular orbit of all the planets, and Mercury the most elliptical after Pluto. Mercury also has the most highly inclined inner planet orbit, tilted at an angle of 7.004° to the ecliptic.

VENUS
Inclination: 3.394°
Eccentricity: 0.007

MARS
Inclination: 1.850°
Eccentricity: 0.093

EARTH
Inclination: 0.000°
Eccentricity: 0.017

MERCURY
Inclination: 7.004°
Eccentricity: 0.206

Sun

THE INNER PLANETS

asteroid belt

JUPITER
Inclination: 1.308°
Eccentricity: 0.048

SATURN
Inclination: 2.488°
Eccentricity: 0.056

URANUS
Inclination: 0.774°
Eccentricity: 0.046

NEPTUNE
Inclination: 1.774°
Eccentricity: 0.010

OUTER PLANETS
The five planets beyond the asteroid belt are Jupiter, Saturn, Uranus, Neptune, and Pluto. The orbit of Pluto is the most unusual of all the planets. It is the most eccentric (it passes inside the orbit of Neptune) and the most inclined, at an angle of 17.15° to the ecliptic.

PLUTO
Inclination: 17.148°
Eccentricity: 0.248

THE OUTER PLANETS

BIRTH OF THE INNER PLANETS

The planets formed 4.6 billion years ago from a vast disk of gas and dust that surrounded the newly forming Sun. The material in the disk began to cool and condense, initially forming grain-sized bodies and then coalescing into the planets as we know them today. Only rocky and metallic materials could survive the immense heat close to the Sun, and the inner planets—Mercury, Venus, Earth, and Mars—still have compositions that reflect this. These planets probably took 100 million years to grow—and another 700 million to mature into the planets that continue to fascinate us.

PLANET-BUILDING TIMES

Event	Duration
Collapse of gas globule to form solar nebula	1–2 million years
Condensation forms first grains	2,000 years
Growth of asteroid-like planetesimals	A few thousand years
Appearance of Moon-size protoplanets	10,000 to 100,000 years
Inner four planets reach half their eventual mass; accretion slows	10 million years
Inner planets reach modern mass; crusts solidify	100 million years
Bombardment modifies planets' crusts	100 to 800 million years
Evolution of planets to present day	3.8 billion years

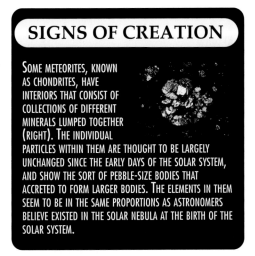
HOT START

Some 4.6 billion years ago, the Earth and all the other planets existed as little more than a thin scattering of gas and grains of dust. The raw material from which the planets sprang probably took the form of a vast disk known to astronomers as the solar nebula.

Like the newly forming Sun, or protosun, that it surrounded, the solar nebula was born when a much larger cloud of gas and dust particles contracted under gravity. Close to the protosun in the center of the solar nebula, temperatures may have been greater than 3,000°F (1,650°C). Eventually, with material in the disk spiraling in to the protosun, the disk grew sparser and its heat was able to escape into space. Then the disk began to cool and its material started to condense, with single atoms grouping together one at a time until they had grown into tiny grains less than a ten-millionth of an inch across.

This process, condensation, was the first step in the planet-building process. Far from the protosun, cooler conditions allowed water, ammonia, and methane to condense into their ice form. But closer in, only rocky and metallic materials could condense.

As the condensed particles orbited the protosun, all swirling in the same direction, some of them began to stick to their neighbors. Astronomers are uncertain what caused the grains to stick together, but it might have been electrostatic forces. Because of this "agglomeration," individual grains grew steadily larger as they merged with adjacent particles.

BOMBARDMENT BEGINS

Within perhaps 2,000 years, the innermost regions of the solar nebula were swarming with countless pebble-size particles. After a few more thousand years, these pebbles had grown to the dimensions of asteroids, with the biggest being miles in diameter. Known as planetesimals, these fragments were by now so large that they grew not only by chance collisions with others, but because they could actually attract their neighbors by virtue of their gravity—a process known as accretion. It was at this point that the planet-building process stepped up another gear.

After about 10 million years, the innermost regions of the disk were populated by four dominant protoplanets that would later become Mercury, Venus, Earth, and Mars, plus maybe one or two others. But by now these objects had mopped up much of the available debris, so their growth rate diminished. It took perhaps another 100 million years for these protoplanets to double in mass to their modern values.

Violent times lay ahead. For some 800 million years—a period known to astronomers as the heavy bombardment phase—the primitive planets continued to sweep up smaller pieces of debris as they orbited around the Sun. Only after this period ended, about 3.8 billion years ago, did the inner planets as we know them truly emerge.

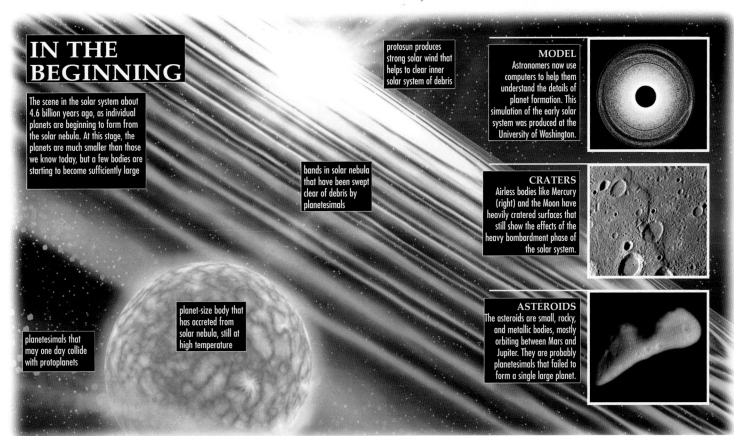

IN THE BEGINNING

The scene in the solar system about 4.6 billion years ago, as individual planets are beginning to form from the solar nebula. At this stage, the planets are much smaller than those we know today, but a few bodies are starting to become sufficiently large

protosun produces strong solar wind that helps to clear inner solar system of debris

bands in solar nebula that have been swept clear of debris by planetesimals

planet-size body that has accreted from solar nebula, still at high temperature

planetesimals that may one day collide with protoplanets

MODEL
Astronomers now use computers to help them understand the details of planet formation. This simulation of the early solar system was produced at the University of Washington.

CRATERS
Airless bodies like Mercury (right) and the Moon have heavily cratered surfaces that still show the effects of the heavy bombardment phase of the solar system.

ASTEROIDS
The asteroids are small, rocky, and metallic bodies, mostly orbiting between Mars and Jupiter. They are probably planetesimals that failed to form a single large planet.

BIRTH OF THE GAS GIANTS

All planets form by accretion—the lumping together of material in a vast spinning disk of dust and gas. But our solar system has planets of two very different kinds. Near the Sun, the four inner planets are small and rocky. Farther out, where conditions were cooler, planets grew from accumulations of snowflakes. In time, they became large enough to attract hydrogen and helium. But the four giant planets—Jupiter, Saturn, Uranus, and Neptune—have differences that are not so easy to explain.

OTHER STARS WITH GIANTS

STAR NAME	LOCATION	PLANET MASS (JUPITER=1)
51 Pegasi	Pegasus	0.4
Upsilon Andromedae	Andromeda	0.7
55 Cancri	Cancer	0.8
Rho Coronae Borealis	Corona Borealis	1.1
16 Cygni B	Cygnus	1.6
Iota Horologii	Horologium	2.2
47 Ursae Majoris	Ursa Major	2.3
Tau Bootis	Bootes	3.6
14 Herculis	Hercules	4.7
70 Virginis	Virgo	7.4

FROM PROTOPLANET TO GIANT

GAS GIANTS
This far from the Sun, protoplanets begin forming around cores of ice. Soon, they are so large that their gravity traps light, fast-moving atoms of hydrogen and helium. They grow until they sweep a clear space along their orbit.

JUPITER
At more than twice the mass of all the other planets, and 1,300 times as large as the Earth, Jupiter is a vast ball of hydrogen and helium around a small core of rock and ice.

At the center of the protoplanetary disk, the Sun is forming. At this stage in the process, it is only a protostar, very much larger than its final size and still collapsing under gravity. It shines dimly, not by nuclear fusion but by the heat released during gravitational contraction.

INNER TERRESTRIALS
Close to the protosun, ice cannot form. But rocky and metallic fragments begin to coalesce to form the inner, terrestrial planets.

HYDROGEN
A cloud of hydrogen gas in the Swan Nebula gives some indication of what our solar system may have looked like before it formed. Hydrogen is by far the most common material in the universe.

70 VIRGINIS
This star has a planet more than seven times the mass of Jupiter. Astronomers suspect that this and other planets found around other stars—all of them very large—are gas giants of the Jovian type.

BIG BABIES

The solar system contains two distinct classes of planet. Huddled close to the Sun are small, dense planets made of rock and metal such as Earth and Mars. But farther out, the planets are much more massive, composed primarily of hydrogen and helium. These outer giants are so large that they contain about 99 percent of the combined mass of all the planets, satellites, and asteroids we know of. How they grew so large, and how the solar system developed these characteristics, is a natural consequence of the way the system was born.

About 4.6 billion years ago, a cloud composed mainly of hydrogen and helium, with water and other ices and particles of carbon dust, began to collapse under its own gravity. As it contracted, the cloud rotated steadily faster. Its material spread into a disk, with the Sun slowly taking shape at its center. At this stage the Sun was not a true star: it had not yet grown massive enough to ignite thermonuclear reactions in its core. It shone only dimly by gravitational contraction—the heat generated when a body shrinks under its own weight. In the disk, gas and dust particles were colliding to form progressively larger objects: grains, boulders, asteroids, and then little protoplanets. Although the Sun was relatively cool, the inner system was still too warm for ice to form. Only rock and metal could contribute to the planet-building process this far in. When these materials were all used up, the innermost protoplanets then stopped growing.

Much farther out in the disk, the planetary nursery was still in full production: the giants were forming. The relatively cool environment meant that outer protoplanets could grow by the accumulation not only of rocky material but also of the plentiful ice—orbiting snowflakes squeezed by gravity into ever-larger snowballs. With so much material on hand, these distant protoplanets grew more massive—several times larger than Earth. By the time the protoplanets that were to become Jupiter and Saturn had grown to fifteen to twenty Earth-masses of material, their gravity was strong enough to haul in the light gases hydrogen and helium.

After one–10 million years, raw material in the disk became scarce. Far beyond Jupiter and Saturn, in the vicinity of Uranus and Neptune, the combination of the rapidly thinning material and the longer orbital timescales meant that these planets could not accumulate as much mass as Jupiter or Saturn had. As a result, they remained as largely ice, without the extensive hydrogen and helium atmospheres of the closer giants.

It was also about this time that the Sun first grew hot enough to become a true star. Very soon, its increasing heat blew any remaining gaseous material in the planetary disk into interstellar space, and the planets effectively stopped growing altogether. The result was the solar system we see today.

ANOMALIES

URANUS AND NEPTUNE ARE FAR LARGER THAN THEORY SAYS THEY OUGHT TO BE. IN THEIR FAR-FLUNG ORBITS, THERE WOULD HAVE BEEN TOO LITTLE MATERIAL FOR THESE PLANETS TO HAVE GROWN TO THEIR PRESENT SIZES. RECENT WORK BY EDWARD THOMMES (ABOVE) AND MARTIN DUNCAN OF QUEENS UNIVERSITY IN KINGSTON, CANADA, SUGGESTS THAT URANUS AND NEPTUNE ACTUALLY FORMED MUCH CLOSER TO THE SUN, NEAR JUPITER. THERE THEY WOULD HAVE BEEN ABLE TO GROW UNTIL JUPITER'S GRAVITY EJECTED THEM AND THEY SETTLED INTO THEIR CURRENT, DISTANT ORBITS.

In this hypothetical image, this backlit ring system of a far-off giant planet makes an impressive sight from its outermost moon, which has a polar orbit.

IMPACTS IN THE SOLAR SYSTEM

Nothing alters a landscape more dramatically than an impact from space. On some worlds, the resulting craters are filled in by erosion or geological processes. But the surfaces of most moons and planets are sterile, and still bear the scars of billions of years of bombardment. Impacts are far less common today than they were in the young solar system. But the vast reservoirs of comets and asteroids still supply plenty of ammunition, and impacts will continue to pound the solar system for billions of years.

BIG HITS

Name	Location	Diameter
Caloris	Mercury	830 miles (1,340 km)
Mead	Venus	180 miles (290 km)
Aitken	Moon	1,560 miles (2,510 km)
Vredefort	Earth	190 miles (310 km)
Hellas Planitia	Mars	1,550 miles (2,500 km)
Valhalla	Callisto	370 miles (600 km)
Herschel	Mimas	80 miles (130 km)
Odysseus	Tethys	250 miles (400 km)
Mazomba	Triton	17 miles (28 km)

STRIKE OUT

At the beginning of the solar system, 4.6 billion years ago, there was little going on except impacts. The planets grew out of the mass of dust that swirled around the young Sun. These particles were welded together by collisions. The impact rate tailed off as more debris was locked away, but on asteroids, moons, and planets, there are still crater scars everywhere.

All impacts are basically explosions. As one body hits another, its velocity is converted into energy. But there are big differences between the craters on various bodies. Impacts on the Moon show a central bowl surrounded by debris or ejecta. In larger craters, the rock is not strong enough to hold a bowl shape, and the crater slumps into a central peak. The craters on Mercury formed in the same way.

But because bodies orbit faster the closer they are to the Sun, these impacts occurred at a higher velocity. Still, the impact ejecta on the Moon sprayed over a wider area—the stronger gravity of Mercury brought it back to the ground before it could travel far.

COMPARING SCARS

On Mars there is another difference. Some of the larger craters sit on splatters that look like the white of a fried egg. These were created as the force of the impact melted subsurface ice. Farther out in the solar system, ice plays an even larger part in shaping impact craters. The moons of Jupiter are mainly ice, and strange craters called palimpsests occur, most dramatically on the moon Ganymede. These are probably ghost craters—impact scars that formed early in the moon's history and have been all but erased by the ice melted through later collisions.

Smaller bodies have not escaped impacts either. The size of the largest crater on an asteroid is a good measure of its strength—some withstand a strike that blasts a hole nearly as large as their diameter without breaking.

Crater counts in a region of a planet or moon are good indicators of the area's age. For example, craters are less common on the Moon's young lava seas than they are on the old highlands. And Venus's low crater score indicates that the planet's surface is only about 500 million years old. The plentiful craters gathered on older surfaces are a sobering reminder of what is to come. Impacts may be less frequent than they were, but the numerous asteroids that continue to roam the solar system promise that one day, the Earth will be back in the crosshairs.

DEATH BY IMPACT

ASTEROID OR COMET IMPACTS HAVE BEEN BLAMED FOR SEVERAL MASS EXTINCTIONS IN THE HISTORY OF LIFE ON EARTH—MOST FAMOUSLY FOR THE DEATH OF THE DINOSAURS, 65 MILLION YEARS AGO. THE IMPACT OCCURRED IN WHAT IS NOW MEXICO, AND LEFT A CRATER OVER 100 MILES (160 KM) ACROSS. BESIDES REGIONAL ANNIHILATION, A COLLISION OF THIS SIZE COULD PUT ENOUGH DUST INTO THE ATMOSPHERE TO BLOCK OUT THE SUN, LEADING TO A GLOBAL FOOD CRISIS.

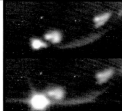

JUPITER STRIKE
The July 1994 collision of Shoemaker-Levy 9 and Jupiter (right) provided a graphic insight to the fallout of a large impact. The strike left Jupiter's gaseous atmosphere with huge impact scars: some larger than the Earth.

MOON BUILDER
A giant impact may have been responsible for forming our own Moon (above). After the Earth formed, it may have been struck by a rogue protoplanet. The collision blasted debris into Earth orbit, which coalesced to form the Moon.

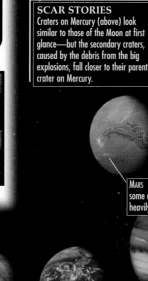

SCAR STORIES
Craters on Mercury (above) look similar to those of the Moon at first glance—but the secondary craters, caused by the debris from the big explosions, fall closer to their parent crater on Mercury.

GRAND SLAMS

Impacts are everywhere in the solar system. Ancient, heavily cratered terrains like the surface of Mercury are the best record of impacts. But even young surfaces have scars.

PLUTO AND CHARON
unknown surfaces

NEPTUNE
heavily cratered moons except for the largest, Triton, which has ice volcanoes

URANUS
cratered icy moons

SATURN
icy surfaces of moons are heavily cratered; crater Herschel on Mimas is one-third of the moon's diameter

MARS
some areas heavily cratered

JUPITER
Jupiter's moon Callisto is the most heavily cratered body in the solar system

VENUS
about 1,000 craters

EARTH
about 150 large craters; Earth's Moon is heavily cratered

MERCURY
heavily cratered

ORBIT CHANGE
Pluto's orbit is elongated compared with the orbits of most other objects in the solar system, and crosses the path of Neptune (right). This erratic course may have been caused by an impact that knocked into Pluto.

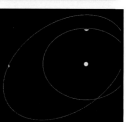

THE SUN

The warmth that you feel on your skin on a sunny day originated in one of the most extreme environments in the entire universe—the nuclear cauldron that lies at the heart of a star. The star in question is the Sun, the body that supplies heat and light to the small planet we call Earth. The way the Sun generates energy in its fiery furnace, and the means by which that energy moves outward from the core to radiate as sunshine on the surface, are the keys to the evolution of life on this planet.

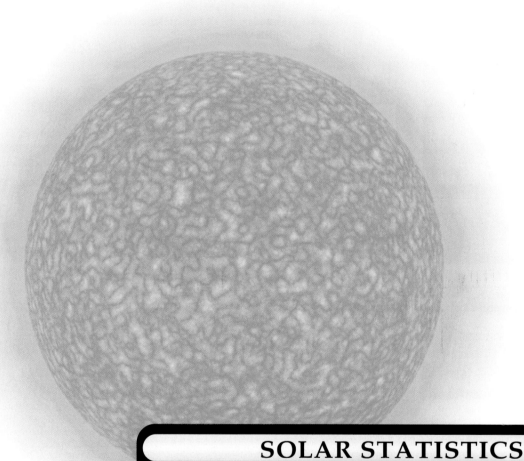

SOLAR STATISTICS

AVERAGE DISTANCE FROM EARTH	92.957 MILLION MILES (149.595 MILLION KM)
DIAMETER	864,950 MILES (1.392 MILLION KM)
AGE	4.5 BILLION YEARS
MASS	1.99 MILLION, TRILLION, TRILLION TONS (1.7 MILLION, TRILLION, TRILLION METRIC TONS)
AVERAGE DENSITY	1.4 TIMES THE DENSITY OF WATER
SURFACE TEMPERATURE	10,900°F (6,040°C)
CORE TEMPERATURE	27 MILLION°F (15 MILLION°C)
COMPOSITION	AT LEAST 90% HYDROGEN, THE REST MOSTLY HELIUM WITH TRACES OF OTHER ELEMENTS

THE SHINING

The Sun is made of gas, mainly hydrogen. But because this body of gas is so massive, the Sun's own gravity creates enormous heat, about 27 million°F (15 million°C), and pressure (3.5 billion megapascals) at the core. Under these conditions, the hydrogen atoms cannot exist in their usual form; they become stripped of their orbiting electrons, leaving just the naked nuclei, called protons.

The heat and pressure agitates these protons to a point where they continually collide with each other. This causes some pairs of hydrogen atoms to fuse together, creating a single atom of a new element—helium. Each time this happens, a minute amount of matter is converted into energy. For each ounce of matter annihilated, enough energy is produced to power a 100W light bulb for about 750,000 years. And in the Sun, some 5 million tons (4,535,924 t) of matter is annihilated every second.

The energy released in these nuclear reactions heats up the core of the Sun still further, and produces high levels of radiation. Photons—tiny "packets" of this radiation—slowly make their way outward from the core through a superdense region called the radiative zone. After that, the photons reach the convective zone where the Sun is less dense and where giant pockets of super-hot gas bubble to the surface.

Eventually, the energy-carrying photons reach the surface and radiate out into space. Much of the energy takes the form of visible light, but there are also infrared light, X-rays, and harmful ultraviolet rays. The light comes from a region known as the photosphere which, effectively, is all we see of the Sun.

The photosphere appears grainy and is constantly moving. The grains seem to come and go, each one lasting some 25 minutes. These 600- to 1,000-mile-wide (1,000- to 1,600-km-wide) "granules" are actually the surface bubbling as energy is carried up from below. The surface of the Sun also shows a larger pattern, called supergranulation. Supergranules are each about 20,000 miles (32,000 km) across, and are related to the massive convection bubbles in the convective zone situated below the Sun's photosphere.

OTHER FEATURES

Above the photosphere is the chromosphere, which can be seen as a pink ring around the Sun during an eclipse. Above this is the corona, from which a hot, thin stream of particles—the solar wind—blows outward into space. Other visible features of the Sun include darker regions called sunspots and bright flares.

The internal workings of the Sun may be complex, but they are nevertheless crucial to our existence. Without them, we would have no light, no energy, and, of course, no life on Earth.

IT'S WHITE

ALTHOUGH THE SUN APPEARS YELLOW WHEN SEEN FROM EARTH, IT IS ACTUALLY WHITE. WE SEE THE SUNLIGHT AFTER IT HAS BEEN FILTERED THROUGH THE EARTH'S ATMOSPHERE. AIR SCATTERS THE BLUE COMPONENT, MAKING THE SKY APPEAR BLUE AND THE SUNLIGHT YELLOW.

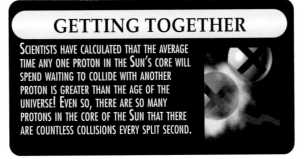

GETTING TOGETHER

SCIENTISTS HAVE CALCULATED THAT THE AVERAGE TIME ANY ONE PROTON IN THE SUN'S CORE WILL SPEND WAITING TO COLLIDE WITH ANOTHER PROTON IS GREATER THAN THE AGE OF THE UNIVERSE! EVEN SO, THERE ARE SO MANY PROTONS IN THE CORE OF THE SUN THAT THERE ARE COUNTLESS COLLISIONS EVERY SPLIT SECOND.

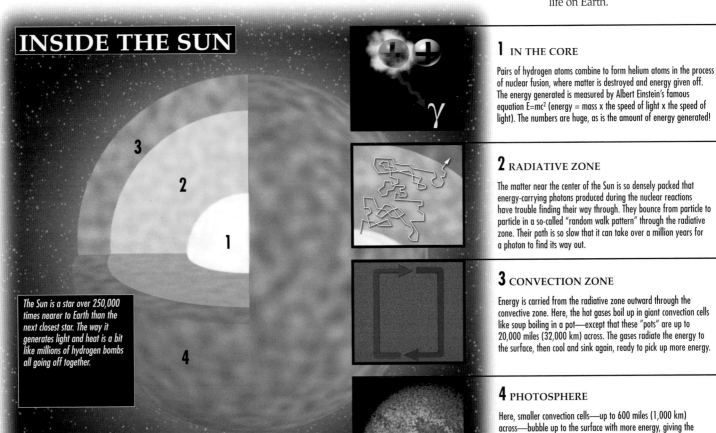

INSIDE THE SUN

The Sun is a star over 250,000 times nearer to Earth than the next closest star. The way it generates light and heat is a bit like millions of hydrogen bombs all going off together.

1 IN THE CORE

Pairs of hydrogen atoms combine to form helium atoms in the process of nuclear fusion, where matter is destroyed and energy given off. The energy generated is measured by Albert Einstein's famous equation $E=mc^2$ (energy = mass x the speed of light x the speed of light). The numbers are huge, as is the amount of energy generated!

2 RADIATIVE ZONE

The matter near the center of the Sun is so densely packed that energy-carrying photons produced during the nuclear reactions have trouble finding their way through. They bounce from particle to particle in a so-called "random walk pattern" through the radiative zone. Their path is so slow that it can take over a million years for a photon to find its way out.

3 CONVECTION ZONE

Energy is carried from the radiative zone outward through the convective zone. Here, the hot gases boil up in giant convection cells like soup boiling in a pot—except that these "pots" are up to 20,000 miles (32,000 km) across. The gases radiate the energy to the surface, then cool and sink again, ready to pick up more energy.

4 PHOTOSPHERE

Here, smaller convection cells—up to 600 miles (1,000 km) across—bubble up to the surface with more energy, giving the surface of the Sun a grainy appearance. The sunshine we see on Earth comes from the photosphere, which is the only part of the Sun we can see directly. The corona and flares are only visible during an eclipse.

ROTATION OF THE SUN

Like the planets, the Sun spins around its axis. But because the Sun is a ball of plasma, not solid like the Earth, its rotation period varies with latitude and depth. The area near the equator moves the fastest, completing a revolution in about 25 days—compared with a revolution taking 35 days at the poles. This latitude variation is detected 30 percent of the way into the Sun, and then there is a change: the core of the Sun seems to rotate more like a rigid body. The Sun's rotation is also linked to the magnetic knots we see as sunspots.

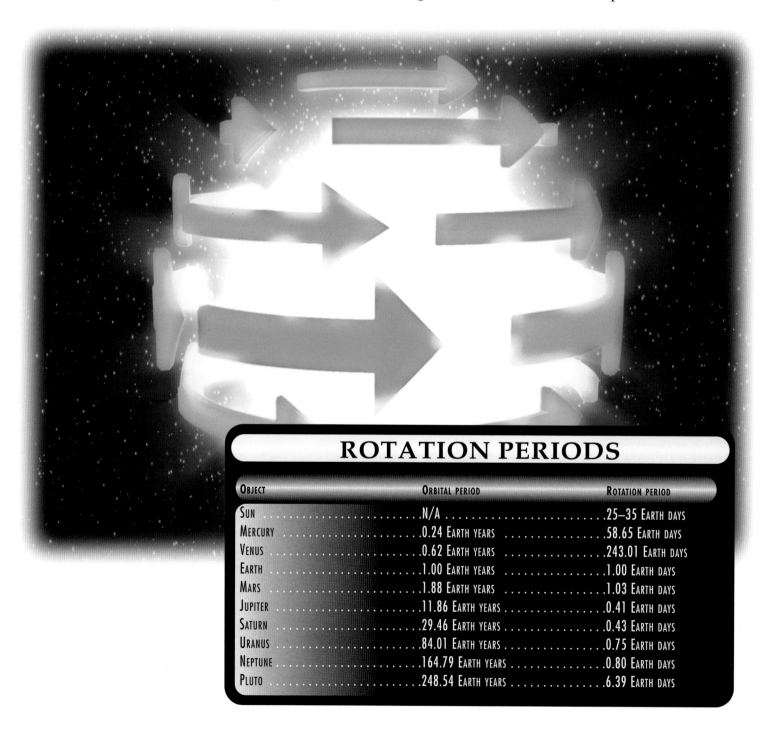

ROTATION PERIODS

Object	Orbital period	Rotation period
Sun	N/A	25–35 Earth days
Mercury	0.24 Earth years	58.65 Earth days
Venus	0.62 Earth years	243.01 Earth days
Earth	1.00 Earth years	1.00 Earth days
Mars	1.88 Earth years	1.03 Earth days
Jupiter	11.86 Earth years	0.41 Earth days
Saturn	29.46 Earth years	0.43 Earth days
Uranus	84.01 Earth years	0.75 Earth days
Neptune	164.79 Earth years	0.80 Earth days
Pluto	248.54 Earth years	6.39 Earth days

TWISTER SUN

The first recorded observations of the Sun's rotation were made about 400 years ago. Among the handful of Europeans at the forefront of this new science was Italian astronomer Galileo Galilei (1564–1642). With his newly invented telescope, he observed dark spots superimposed on the solar disk and suggested that they were physically associated with the Sun itself—they were not, as was previously believed, dark clouds or planets situated between us and the Sun. It was a simple step to measure the time it took for these spots—now called sunspots—to move across the solar disk. Galileo found that the Sun's "day" was a little under one month long.

But there were problems. As more astronomers carried out the same experiment, it became clear that the Sun's rotation rate was difficult to calculate exactly. Sometimes the spots appeared to move quickly across the Sun, and at other times they moved quite slowly. It was not until the mid-nineteenth century that English astronomer Richard Carrington (1826–75) found the answer to the puzzle. In 1863, he observed that the solar equator was spinning once every 27 days as seen from Earth, but that at a latitude roughly halfway to the poles, the period was closer to 30 days. The Sun's rotation rate does indeed vary with latitude, and shows a smooth variation in spin period from 25 days at the equator to 35 days or even more at the poles. This rotation at different speeds is known as differential rotation. It is also seen in the gas planets of our solar system and in spiral galaxies.

THE SUN'S HUM

More recently, with the advent of helioseismology, astronomers have been able to see how the Sun rotates internally. Just as the study of earthquakes, or seismology, reveals properties about our planet's interior, so the study of vibrations on the Sun—helioseismology—offers clues to the interior of the solar furnace. The Sun is a violent place, so it is also very noisy. The sound waves that carry this noise move through the Sun and change direction when they encounter regions of different density. This process is similar to the bending of light rays when

they cross the boundary between water and air, an effect that makes swimming pools appear shallower than they really are. When the sound waves reach the Sun's surface, they cause it to pulsate. By observing these pulsations, astronomers can make accurate deductions about the interior movements of the Sun.

The results suggest that the convective zone—the outer layer of the Sun—has the same rotation pattern as the surface. Near the boundary region between the convective zone and the deeper radiative zone, the Sun starts to show a difference in rotation rate with depth. The equatorial rotation speed decreases while the polar

rotation rate increases. The rates equalize around 40 percent of the way into the Sun. From here on in, the Sun rotates as a rigid body. The exact period is uncertain, but it appears to spin roughly once every 25 days.

What happens at even greater depths, though, is a mystery. Because the deepest sound waves suffer the most modifications in their journey to the surface, the information that they carry about the deep interior is easily drowned out. To study the Sun's core requires much more sensitive equipment than that currently available, and is a puzzle that future generations of astronomers will have to face.

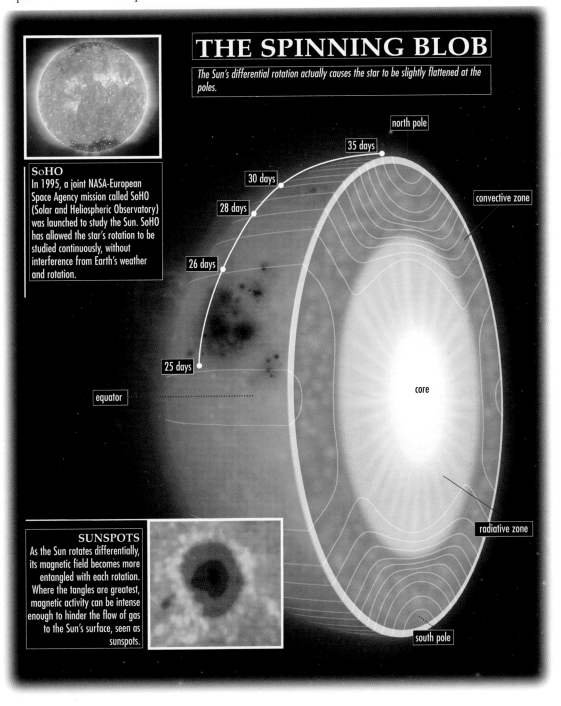

THE SPINNING BLOB

The Sun's differential rotation actually causes the star to be slightly flattened at the poles.

north pole

35 days

30 days

28 days

26 days

25 days

convective zone

core

radiative zone

equator

south pole

SoHO
In 1995, a joint NASA-European Space Agency mission called SoHO (Solar and Heliospheric Observatory) was launched to study the Sun. SoHO has allowed the star's rotation to be studied continuously, without interference from Earth's weather and rotation.

SUNSPOTS
As the Sun rotates differentially, its magnetic field becomes more entangled with each rotation. Where the tangles are greatest, magnetic activity can be intense enough to hinder the flow of gas to the Sun's surface, seen as sunspots.

SOLAR ECLIPSES

A total eclipse occurs when the Moon passes between the Earth and the Sun, blotting out the Sun's disk entirely and turning day into night. Throughout history, few natural phenomena have filled the human race with such awe. Even for professional astronomers, the sudden and dramatic darkening of the Sun, accompanied by a spectacular range of optical effects, is an experience never to be forgotten. But eclipses are not just entertaining—they also enable us to examine features of the Sun that are invisible at other times.

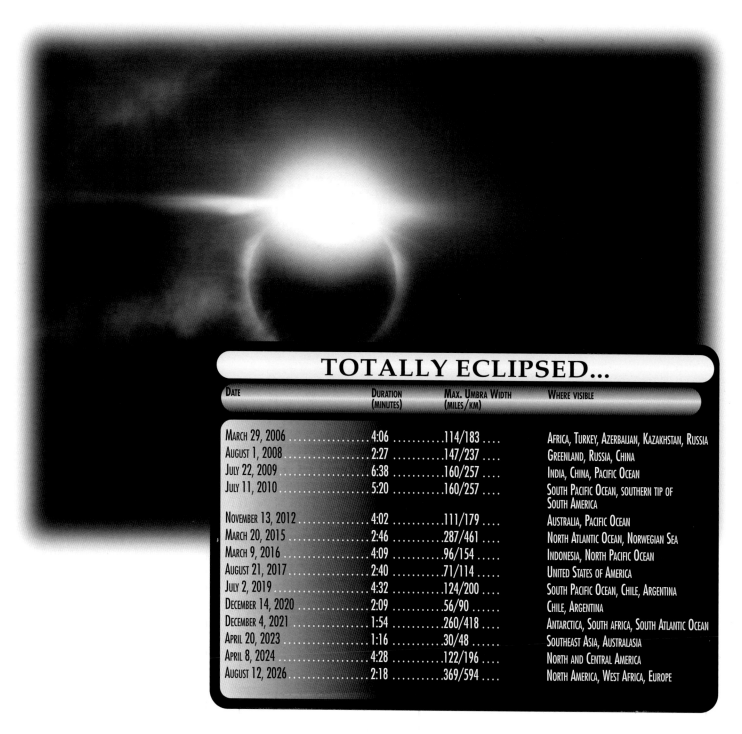

TOTALLY ECLIPSED...

Date	Duration (minutes)	Max. Umbra Width (miles/km)	Where visible
MARCH 29, 2006	4:06	114/183	AFRICA, TURKEY, AZERBAIJAN, KAZAKHSTAN, RUSSIA
AUGUST 1, 2008	2:27	147/237	GREENLAND, RUSSIA, CHINA
JULY 22, 2009	6:38	160/257	INDIA, CHINA, PACIFIC OCEAN
JULY 11, 2010	5:20	160/257	SOUTH PACIFIC OCEAN, SOUTHERN TIP OF SOUTH AMERICA
NOVEMBER 13, 2012	4:02	111/179	AUSTRALIA, PACIFIC OCEAN
MARCH 20, 2015	2:46	287/461	NORTH ATLANTIC OCEAN, NORWEGIAN SEA
MARCH 9, 2016	4:09	96/154	INDONESIA, NORTH PACIFIC OCEAN
AUGUST 21, 2017	2:40	71/114	UNITED STATES OF AMERICA
JULY 2, 2019	4:32	124/200	SOUTH PACIFIC OCEAN, CHILE, ARGENTINA
DECEMBER 14, 2020	2:09	56/90	CHILE, ARGENTINA
DECEMBER 4, 2021	1:54	260/418	ANTARCTICA, SOUTH AFRICA, SOUTH ATLANTIC OCEAN
APRIL 20, 2023	1:16	30/48	SOUTHEAST ASIA, AUSTRALASIA
APRIL 8, 2024	4:28	122/196	NORTH AND CENTRAL AMERICA
AUGUST 12, 2026	2:18	369/594	NORTH AMERICA, WEST AFRICA, EUROPE

DARKNESS IN THE DAYTIME

As the Moon orbits the Earth every month or so, it reaches a point at which it is in roughly the same direction as the Sun when seen from Earth. From this you might imagine that a total eclipse of the Sun would be a monthly event—but as we know, it is actually quite rare.

Partial eclipses, where just part of the Sun is obscured by the Moon, are infrequent enough. In most years there are between two and four, although in 1935 there were five. Total eclipses are rarer still: there are seldom more than about seventy per century.

The infrequency of eclipses is largely explained by the angle of the Moon's orbit around the Earth, and by the size of the Moon relative to the Sun. The Moon's orbit is at about 5° relative to the orbit of the Earth around the Sun. This means that the Moon does not pass over the face of the Sun every time it orbits the Earth. The Moon is also relatively small, which means that its shadow often misses the Earth altogether.

When the Moon does cast its shadow on the Earth, its path crosses the Earth in a general west-to-east direction. Those fortunate enough to be lining the route are in for a spectacular show.

It takes several hours for the eclipse to unfold—a sequence of events that astronomers call contacts. Each point along the path sees exactly the same thing, but at a later time of day the farther east you go. For this reason some dedicated eclipse watchers take to aircraft, in an effort to chase the eclipse around the globe.

ANATOMY OF AN ECLIPSE

The first stage of an eclipse, called first contact, occurs when the Moon appears to touch the edge of the Sun. The eclipse is now in its partial phase. Second contact, or totality, starts at the instant the Moon is completely in front of the Sun and usually lasts no more than a few minutes. Third contact is when the Sun is just about to be revealed again. From then on the eclipse reverts to being partial until, at fourth contact, the Moon clears the Sun's disk completely. Because the Sun is so bright, there is no noticeable reduction in daylight until some 80 percent of it is covered. But toward second contact, an eerie darkness begins to descend with increasing rapidity.

In ancient times, people reported that the ground became filled with "writhing snakes." We now know that these mysterious serpents are, in fact, moving bands of shadow—the result of the Sun's narrowing crescent being focused by turbulence in the air.

NIGHT AND DAY

Despite the darkness, the path of an eclipse is narrow enough for light to remain visible on the horizon. Stars appear overhead and the air temperature becomes several degrees cooler.

As the bright disk of the Sun becomes obscured, the dimmer reddish prominences and outer layer, or chromosphere, become visible. Beyond them is the Sun's corona, which appears as a halo of bright, white light around the black disk of the Moon and is a truly awe-inspiring sight. For those lucky enough to watch, it is an unforgettable experience.

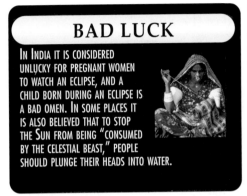

BAD LUCK

In India it is considered unlucky for pregnant women to watch an eclipse, and a child born during an eclipse is a bad omen. In some places it is also believed that to stop the Sun from being "consumed by the celestial beast," people should plunge their heads into water.

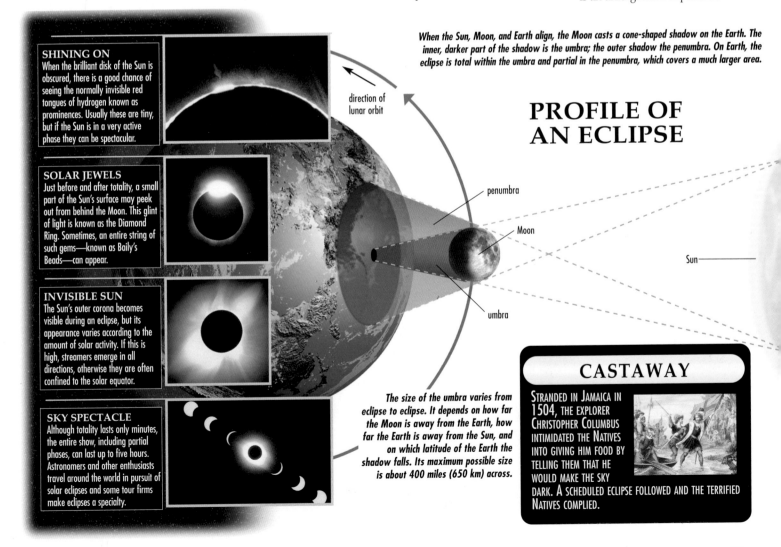

When the Sun, Moon, and Earth align, the Moon casts a cone-shaped shadow on the Earth. The inner, darker part of the shadow is the umbra; the outer shadow the penumbra. On Earth, the eclipse is total within the umbra and partial in the penumbra, which covers a much larger area.

SHINING ON
When the brilliant disk of the Sun is obscured, there is a good chance of seeing the normally invisible red tongues of hydrogen known as prominences. Usually these are tiny, but if the Sun is in a very active phase they can be spectacular.

SOLAR JEWELS
Just before and after totality, a small part of the Sun's surface may peek out from behind the Moon. This glint of light is known as the Diamond Ring. Sometimes, an entire string of such gems—known as Baily's Beads—can appear.

INVISIBLE SUN
The Sun's outer corona becomes visible during an eclipse, but its appearance varies according to the amount of solar activity. If this is high, streamers emerge in all directions, otherwise they are often confined to the solar equator.

SKY SPECTACLE
Although totality lasts only minutes, the entire show, including partial phases, can last up to five hours. Astronomers and other enthusiasts travel around the world in pursuit of solar eclipses and some tour firms make eclipses a specialty.

direction of lunar orbit

PROFILE OF AN ECLIPSE

penumbra

Moon

Sun

umbra

The size of the umbra varies from eclipse to eclipse. It depends on how far the Moon is away from the Earth, how far the Earth is away from the Sun, and on which latitude of the Earth the shadow falls. Its maximum possible size is about 400 miles (650 km) across.

CASTAWAY
Stranded in Jamaica in 1504, the explorer Christopher Columbus intimidated the Natives into giving him food by telling them that he would make the sky dark. A scheduled eclipse followed and the terrified Natives complied.

SUNSPOTS

The Sun is a far from perfect star. Its surface is blemished by sunspots—gigantic blotches, often larger in diameter than the Earth, where the temperature is 3,500°F (2,000°C) cooler than the surrounding area. Sunspots usually occur in groups, up to one hundred at a time, which can last from half a day to several weeks when the Sun's magnetic field is affected by its uneven rotation. But despite the vast range of their size and duration, and their dark appearance, all occur in active zones where the Sun's seething magnetic activity penetrates the outermost layer of hot gas, its photosphere. Through these sunspot windows we can see the soul of the Sun.

SUNSPOT FACTS

Penumbra Temperature	9,400°F (5,200°C)
Umbra Temperature	6,400°F (3,500°C)
Typical Sunspot Diameter	8,000 miles (13,000 km), or the Earth's diameter
Minimum Diameter of Sunspot Visible to the Naked Eye	27,152 miles (43,696 km), or seven times the Earth's diameter
Typical Sunspot Lifetime	A few days
Shortest-ever Sunspot Lifetime	Less than an hour
Longest-ever Sunspot Group Lifetime	200 days
Earliest Recorded Sunspot Sighting	800 bce in China

IMPERFECT STAR

When Chinese astronomers saw dark spots on the Sun's disk one sunset 2,800 years ago, they had no real explanation. The great Italian astronomer Galileo Galilei claimed that he first saw the strange markings in 1610. He wisely protected his eyesight by projecting the image of the Sun from his new telescope onto a card, and was the first to realize that the marks were on the "spotty and impure" solar globe itself. But it took a twentieth-century science called spectroscopy to show that sunspots are a by-product of the Sun's magnetism. Spectroscopy is the tool that reveals what stars are made of. Each element in the Sun's atmosphere absorbs light of certain wavelengths. So if sunlight is split into its spectrum of component colors, the missing wavelengths leave dark lines—showing which elements are in the Sun.

WILDLY ATTRACTED

Often, light can give more information. In 1908, the American astronomer George Hale (1868–1938) noticed that the "signature" lines in the spectrum split in the presence of sunspots. Where there should have been one spectral line, he saw several. This phenomenon was known to occur in the presence of a strong magnetic field. Hale concluded that sunspots are vast regions of magnetic turmoil where the Sun's own magnetic field can be up to a thousand times stronger than its average level.

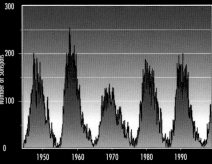

WHAT'S IN A SUNSPOT?

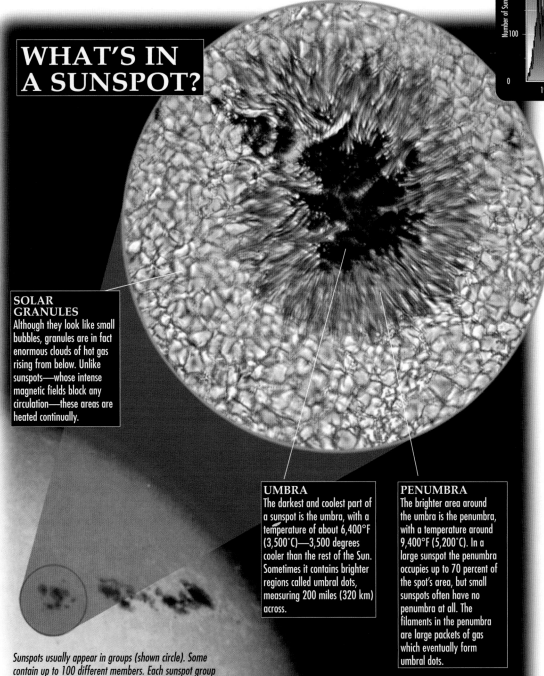

SOLAR GRANULES
Although they look like small bubbles, granules are in fact enormous clouds of hot gas rising from below. Unlike sunspots—whose intense magnetic fields block any circulation—these areas are heated continually.

UMBRA
The darkest and coolest part of a sunspot is the umbra, with a temperature of about 6,400°F (3,500°C)—3,500 degrees cooler than the rest of the Sun. Sometimes it contains brighter regions called umbral dots, measuring 200 miles (320 km) across.

PENUMBRA
The brighter area around the umbra is the penumbra, with a temperature around 9,400°F (5,200°C). In a large sunspot the penumbra occupies up to 70 percent of the spot's area, but small sunspots often have no penumbra at all. The filaments in the penumbra are large packets of gas which eventually form umbral dots.

Sunspots usually appear in groups (shown circle). Some contain up to 100 different members. Each sunspot group may last for months.

Part of the disruption comes from the Sun's own rotation. It spins just as the Earth does, completing a full turn in a month. But the Sun is not solid; its equator turns faster than its poles. This so-called differential rotation plays havoc with the solar magnetic field.

Magnetic field lines spanning the Sun resemble sections of an orange. The Sun pulls these vertical lines around with it as it spins. Since the Sun spins fastest at its equator, the lines begin to stretch and eventually become so twisted that they poke out of the Sun's outer layers, its photosphere, and form huge loops.

Sunspots occur at the bases of these magnetic loops—just where theory would predict them. Astronomers believe that the loops inhibit charged particles of hot gas and so prevent them from carrying heat to the surface. Cut off from this circulation, areas at the base of loops grow much cooler—and darker—than the rest of the photosphere. We see these shaded areas as sunspots.

Theory also predicts that magnetic fields will tend to tangle most around the equator. Again, this is exactly what observations show: sunspots do indeed appear to migrate from high to low latitudes on a timescale of about eleven years. The only question that remains is why, exactly, the process should take eleven years.

25

MERCURY

Barren Mercury, the first planet out from the Sun, is a small, rocky world that is scarred by impact craters and scorched by solar radiation almost seven times fiercer than that on Earth. With no substantial atmosphere to counteract the Sun's rays, the surface can reach a searing 800°F (420°C)

during the day and plunge to –290°F (–140°C) at night. But the near-vacuum on the surface of Mercury has also helped to preserve the planet's contours, and the imprints left there by countless meteoroid scars have provided valuable information about the early days of the solar system.

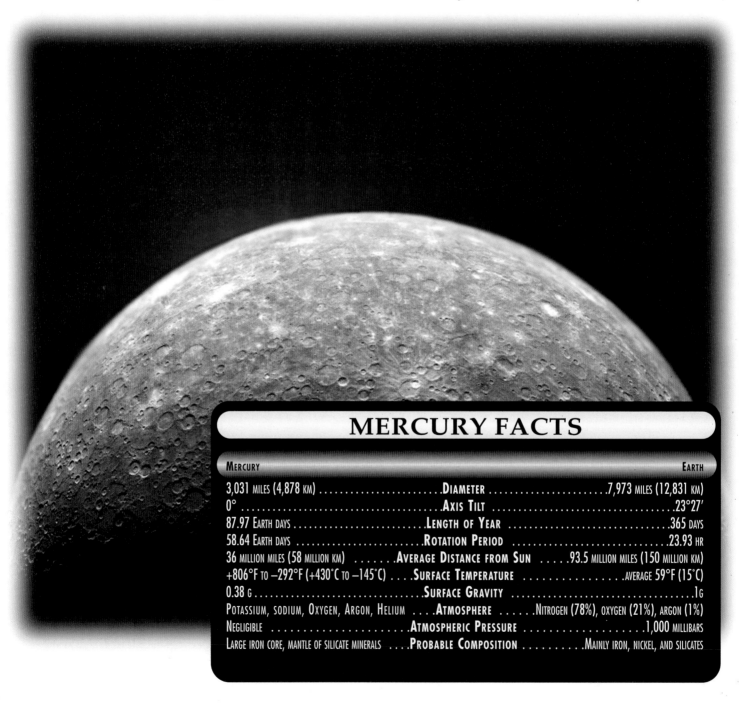

MERCURY FACTS

Mercury		Earth
3,031 miles (4,878 km)	Diameter	7,973 miles (12,831 km)
0°	Axis Tilt	23°27'
87.97 Earth days	Length of Year	365 days
58.64 Earth days	Rotation Period	23.93 hr
36 million miles (58 million km)	Average Distance from Sun	93.5 million miles (150 million km)
+806°F to –292°F (+430°C to –145°C)	Surface Temperature	average 59°F (15°C)
0.38 g	Surface Gravity	1g
Potassium, sodium, Oxygen, Argon, Helium	Atmosphere	Nitrogen (78%), oxygen (21%), argon (1%)
Negligible	Atmospheric Pressure	1,000 millibars
Large iron core, mantle of silicate minerals	Probable Composition	Mainly iron, nickel, and silicates

SUNBURN AND SCARS

At first sight, Mercury has more in common with the Moon than with any major planets. Both share jagged, impact-scarred landscapes, thanks to the absence of wind and water that softened the contours of the Earth and Mars. Mercury is also close to the Moon in size, a little under one and a half times larger. This is significantly smaller than both Jupiter's moon Ganymede and Saturn's moon Titan.

Yet Mercury is much denser than the Moon, and apart from the Earth itself, it is the densest body in the solar system. Scientists believe this is explained by a massive body of iron at the planet's core. In fact, the Earth may only be denser than Mercury because of its superior mass, which increases the strength of its gravitational field and pulls it together more tightly. It is possible that Mercury's iron core accounts for most of the planet's interior.

Pressures and temperatures at Mercury's core are likely to be so high that at least some of the iron remains permanently liquid. Further evidence for this comes from Mercury's magnetic field, which is much stronger than those of Venus and Mars, but only about 1 percent as strong as Earth's. Scientists believe that the magnetic fields of all the rocky inner planets are generated by ripples in the molten metal at their cores.

MYSTERIES OF THE PLAINS

Mercury's surface is not totally peppered with craters: there are also smoother plains, like the seas of the Moon. No one is sure how these plains were formed. One theory is that after cataclysmic impacts like the one that created the mighty Caloris Basin, lava from the planet's molten interior gushed out over the surface. Other plains may consist of matter sprayed out after meteoroid impacts.

With no erosion by wind and water and no tectonic plates to shift and crumple, Mercury has never experienced the natural forces that constantly reshape the Earth. As a result, the pattern of impacts provides important clues to the evolution of the solar system. When Mercury's plains were formed, they provided a fresh surface for impacts. But the largest craters on Mercury are found only in the older, more rugged regions that predate the plains, which suggests that massive impacts by interplanetary debris were a regular occurrence during the early days of the solar system, but that by the time Mercury's plains were formed, they had petered out.

Mercury's most unusual features are the huge ridges or scarps that snake across the surface—sometimes for over 100 miles (160 km)—and rise to nearly 10,000 feet (3,000 meters) above the surrounding landscape. These wrinkles are a sign that Mercury once shrank by over 3,000 feet (900 m)—0.1 percent of the planet's surface area—as the core cooled.

Because it is so close to the Sun, Mercury is difficult and dangerous to observe. Little was known about Mercury until the *Mariner 10* probe visited in the mid-1970s, but the planet's slow rotation allowed *Mariner 10* to map only 40 percent of the surface. Recently, the *MESSENGER* probe completed its full map of Mercury, with further data still being analyzed.

SUN DANCE

A "DAY" ON MERCURY IS UNLIKE ANY OTHER IN THE SOLAR SYSTEM: IT LASTS TWO YEARS, AND THE SUN REGULARLY APPEARS TO MOVE BACKWARD IN THE SKY. THE REASON IS MERCURY'S UNIQUE COMBINATION OF SLOW ROTATION ABOUT ITS AXIS AND RAPID PERIOD OF ORBIT AROUND THE SUN. TOGETHER, THESE EXTEND THE MERCURIAN "SOLAR DAY"—FROM NOON TO NOON—TO 176 EARTH DAYS, OR TWO MERCURIAN YEARS. FROM CERTAIN SPOTS ON THE PLANET ONE WOULD SEE THE SUN RISE, THEN DIP BACK BELOW THE HORIZON BEFORE RISING FOR GOOD. SIMILARLY, OTHER POINTS ON MERCURY WOULD WITNESS A "DOUBLE SUNSET."

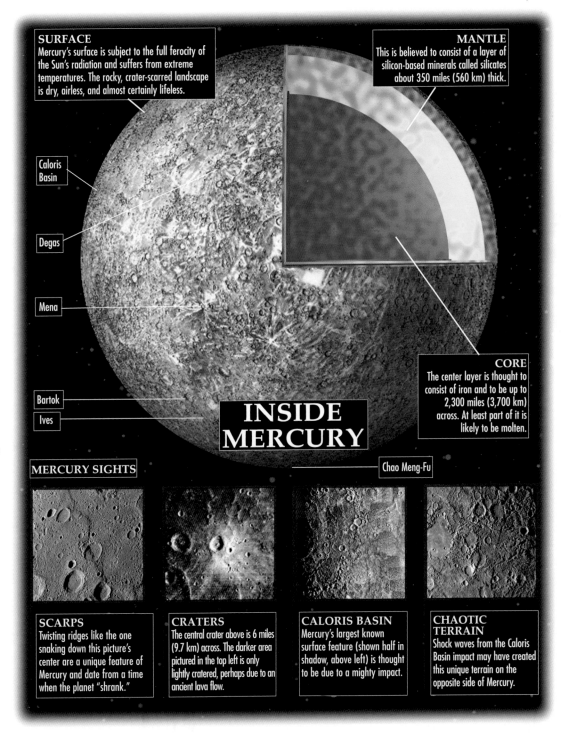

INSIDE MERCURY

SURFACE
Mercury's surface is subject to the full ferocity of the Sun's radiation and suffers from extreme temperatures. The rocky, crater-scarred landscape is dry, airless, and almost certainly lifeless.

MANTLE
This is believed to consist of a layer of silicon-based minerals called silicates about 350 miles (560 km) thick.

CORE
The center layer is thought to consist of iron and to be up to 2,300 miles (3,700 km) across. At least part of it is likely to be molten.

Caloris Basin

Degas

Mena

Bartok

Ives

Chao Meng-Fu

MERCURY SIGHTS

SCARPS
Twisting ridges like the one snaking down this picture's center are a unique feature of Mercury and date from a time when the planet "shrank."

CRATERS
The central crater above is 6 miles (9.7 km) across. The darker area pictured in the top left is only lightly cratered, perhaps due to an ancient lava flow.

CALORIS BASIN
Mercury's largest known surface feature (shown half in shadow, above left) is thought to be due to a mighty impact.

CHAOTIC TERRAIN
Shock waves from the Caloris Basin impact may have created this unique terrain on the opposite side of Mercury.

VENUS

Venus, the second planet from the Sun, is similar to the Earth in size and mass. But there the resemblance ends. Both planets formed at about the same time from similar materials, and once had similar atmospheres. Now, Venus is dry and lifeless with not a trace of water on its surface, but the Earth teems with life and over two-thirds of it is covered in oceans. Searing temperatures, crushing pressures, and a suffocating atmosphere have made Venus a very different world from our own.

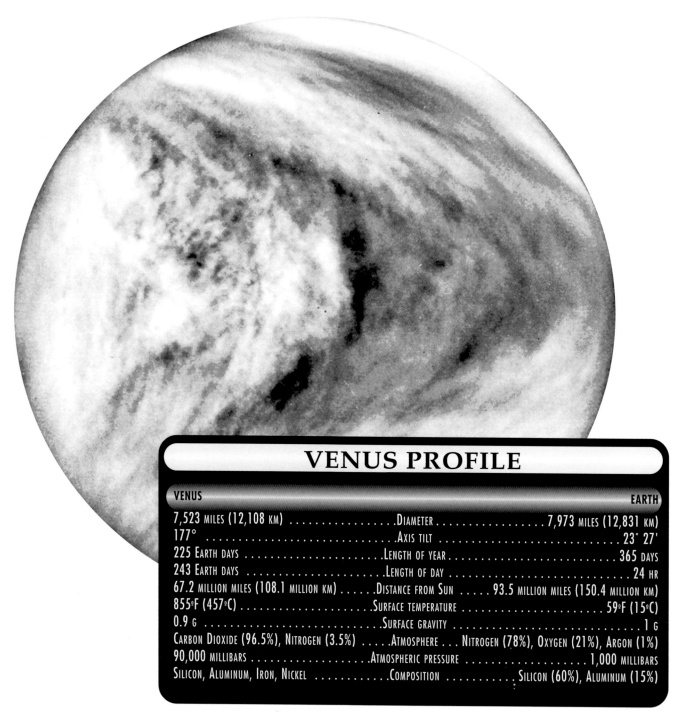

VENUS PROFILE

VENUS		EARTH
7,523 MILES (12,108 KM)	Diameter	7,973 MILES (12,831 KM)
177°	Axis tilt	23° 27'
225 EARTH DAYS	Length of year	365 DAYS
243 EARTH DAYS	Length of day	24 HR
67.2 MILLION MILES (108.1 MILLION KM)	Distance from Sun	93.5 MILLION MILES (150.4 MILLION KM)
855°F (457°C)	Surface temperature	59°F (15°C)
0.9 G	Surface gravity	1 G
CARBON DIOXIDE (96.5%), NITROGEN (3.5%)	Atmosphere	NITROGEN (78%), OXYGEN (21%), ARGON (1%)
90,000 MILLIBARS	Atmospheric pressure	1,000 MILLIBARS
SILICON, ALUMINUM, IRON, NICKEL	Composition	SILICON (60%), ALUMINUM (15%)

A BARREN WASTELAND

Our knowledge of the cloud-shrouded surface of Venus comes from radar images produced by Earth-based radio telescopes and orbiting spacecraft. These images have revealed a landscape of massive volcanoes, surrounded by extensive lava plains crossed by lava flow channels thousands of miles long. The few impact craters are large, because only the most massive meteorites have been able to penetrate the atmosphere. Volcanic activity may still be occurring here and there, and the curious blisterlike features called coronae are believed to be bulges caused by heat within the planet melting and blistering the crust.

Venus's huge number of volcanoes seems puzzling at first, given its resemblance to the Earth. From measurements of the gravitational field of Venus, scientists conclude that the planet has an iron core, about the same size as the Earth's, overlaid by a rocky mantle, again just like that of the Earth. Both planets should produce about the same amount of internal heat, largely from the decay of radioactive elements. So why, then, is the surface of Venus dominated by volcanoes while the Earth's is not?

The explanation may lie in a crucial difference revealed by radar mapping from the *Magellan* spacecraft. Where the Earth's crust is fractured into constantly moving "plates," with earthquakes and volcanoes occurring along their margins, the crust of Venus seems to be intact. Instead of internal heat being lost through volcanoes at plate margins, as it is on Earth, it is thought to escape through the numerous "hot spot" volcanoes that cover the surface of Venus.

Scientists think that the original atmospheres of both Venus and the Earth were created from gases released by volcanoes when both planets were very young and volcanic activity was much more intense. But the closeness of Venus to the Sun meant that the "greenhouse effect," in which heat is trapped within the atmosphere, resulted in the temperature rising so high that all the remaining surface water evaporated.

With all the water now in the atmosphere, the intense ultraviolet radiation from the Sun split the water molecules into hydrogen and oxygen. The hydrogen escaped into space and the oxygen combined with other chemicals in the atmosphere. So eventually, Venus lost virtually all its water.

In contrast, the Earth cooled down, oceans formed, and life began to develop. The Earth became a living planet while Venus remained barren.

TRANSIT

In 1769, observers watching Venus pass in front of the Sun saw that it appeared elongated as it crossed the edge of the Sun's disk. It was later realized that this could only have happened if Venus had an atmosphere.

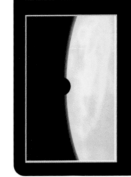 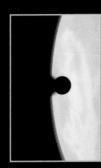 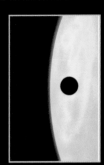

HOT PROBE

The temperatures and pressures on Venus are so extreme that the first three probes that were sent into the atmosphere were destroyed on the way down. *Venera 7* was the first to land safely, in December 1970, but its signals were lost after 23 minutes.

Aphrodite Terra

Atalanta Planitia

North Pole

Beta Regio

Tethys Regio

Ishtar Terra

Lakshmi Planum

Cleopatra Patera

Maxwell Montes

Gula Mons

Eistla Regio

SURFACE FEATURES

RIFT VALLEYS
The large rift valley in the west of the Eistla Regio area is an indication of past movements in the crust. It was formed when two parts of the crust moved apart and the ground between them sank.

RADAR MAP
Although the surface of Venus is shrouded with clouds, its features can be mapped with radar. This map was based on data gathered by the *Magellan* radar-mapping spacecraft that went into orbit around Venus in 1990.

MOUNTAIN HIGH
Gula Mons, an extinct volcano in the western Eistla Regio area, rises about 9,800 feet (3,000 m) above the surrounding plains.

EARTH

The blue-green Earth is the only place in the solar system known to have large quantities of water in liquid form. Water was almost certainly a prerequisite for Earth's unique characteristic among the solar system and even the universe: its living things. Life on Earth is responsible for its unusual atmosphere, rich in the highly reactive gas oxygen. Earth is the birthplace and current sole residence of a race of intelligent bipeds. Recently, spacecraft built by these humans have allowed them to see their planet from space—and recognize its place in the solar system and beyond.

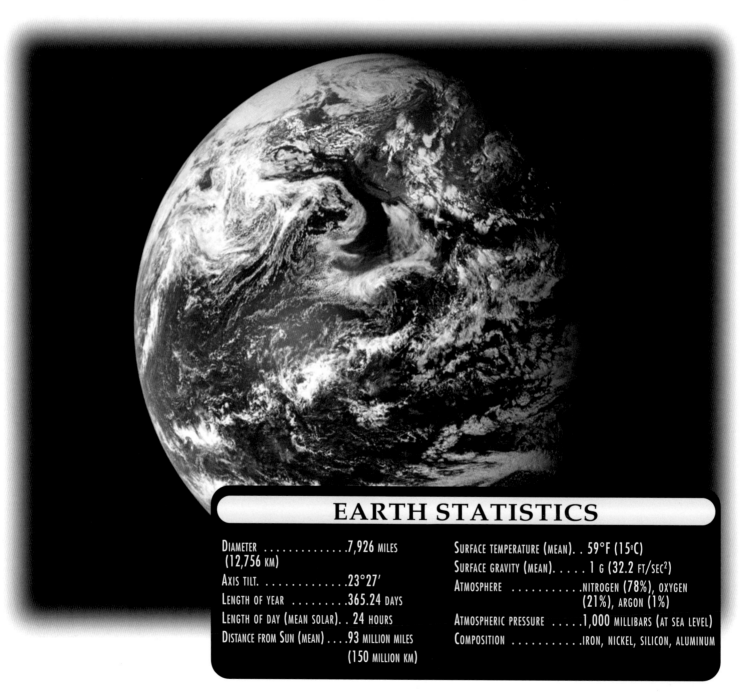

EARTH STATISTICS

DIAMETER . . . . .7,926 MILES (12,756 KM)	SURFACE TEMPERATURE (MEAN). . 59°F (15°C)
AXIS TILT. . . . . .23°27'	SURFACE GRAVITY (MEAN). . . . . 1 G (32.2 FT/SEC²)
LENGTH OF YEAR . . . . .365.24 DAYS	ATMOSPHERE . . . . .NITROGEN (78%), OXYGEN (21%), ARGON (1%)
LENGTH OF DAY (MEAN SOLAR). . 24 HOURS	ATMOSPHERIC PRESSURE . . . . .1,000 MILLIBARS (AT SEA LEVEL)
DISTANCE FROM SUN (MEAN) . . . .93 MILLION MILES (150 MILLION KM)	COMPOSITION . . . . .IRON, NICKEL, SILICON, ALUMINUM

LIVING WORLD

Of the four rocky worlds that make up the inner solar system, Earth is probably the only one that is still geologically active—4.5 billion years after its formation. Vast, continent-sized plates of crustal rock float on top of molten magma, continually replenished by new material that pushes upward along mid-ocean ridges from the planet's interior. These plates push powerfully against each other, forcing up new mountain ranges and constantly rebuilding the planet's surface.

Earth's living geology is one reason why the planet bears so few of the craters that mark the faces of the other inner planets and the Earth's own Moon. Back in the early years of the solar system, Earth must have received its fair share of the asteroid bombardments that scar its neighbors to this day. But crustal movement has long since healed the damage and replaced any impact craters with new landscapes.

In any case, on Earth both meteoric craters and new-created mountains are under attack by erosion as soon as they form. The planet's surface is dominated by a vast blanket of liquid water, which is several miles deep on average. The Earth's water is a powerful scouring force, especially coupled with the winds that are a constant feature of its atmosphere. The atmosphere itself is far less dense than that of neighboring planet Venus. But coupled with the Earth's

pronounced axial tilt and its speedy, 24-hour daily rotation, it is more than enough to give the planet powerful weather systems that are visible as swirling cloud patterns from far off in space.

It is the composition of Earth's atmosphere, rather than its density, that distinguishes it from Mars and Venus. Earth's air is 21 percent oxygen, a reactive gas discernible only in minute quantities elsewhere in the solar system. There are also traces of other gases—notably methane—that should not be able to coexist for long with oxygen. And carbon dioxide, the major component of the atmospheres of Mars and Venus, exists only as a few hundred parts per million—just enough to provide a modest greenhouse effect. Oxygen provides energy for the Earth's extraordinary array of life—and is in turn renewed by the plants that depend on it.

The unusual atmosphere is a clear indication of the Earth's most remarkable feature: life. The first microorganisms appeared more than 3.5 billion years ago, and ever since then, they have been at work on the Earth's atmosphere—and a lot of other things, too. Living organisms are almost certainly responsible for the high oxygen content of the air,

which without constant replenishment would soon be locked up in chemical oxides, just as on Mars and Venus. Over time, life has diversified into millions of genetically diverse species, some of which can exist in even the most inhospitable terrestrial environments.

One of Earth's life-forms has even found ways of sending itself or its artifacts outside the atmosphere: a few have escaped Earth's gravity altogether. But it is too early to say whether Earth life will prove an entirely local phenomenon, or whether it will spread throughout the solar system and even across interstellar space to other stars. With other planets or celestial bodies potentially able to sustain life, perhaps one day evolution will result in life on Mars.

TWIN PLANET

THE EARTH'S OVERSIZED SATELLITE IS A SOLAR SYSTEM ODDITY. WHEREAS MOST PLANETARY MOONS ARE A TINY FRACTION OF THEIR PRIMARY'S DIMENSIONS, THE MOON IS MORE THAN A QUARTER OF THE EARTH'S DIAMETER—THOUGH LESS THAN 2 PERCENT OF ITS MASS. SEEN FROM DEEP SPACE, THE EARTH-MOON SYSTEM APPEARS ALMOST AS A DOUBLE PLANET—AS IS STRIKINGLY APPARENT IN THIS PICTURE TAKEN BY THE *GALILEO* SPACECRAFT IN 1992, 4 MILLION MILES (6.5 MILLION KM) OUTBOUND ON ITS WAY TO JUPITER.

INSIDE OUT
Magma from the Hawaiian volcano of Kilauea flows into the sea in an explosion of sparks (above). Such outbursts of lava—which can reach temperatures of up to 3,500°F (1,920°C)—can transform landscapes very quickly.

COLD POLES
Because the Earth's axial tilt restricts the sunlight falling on the poles, both are covered with ice. Antarctica's ice sheet (right) is up to 3 miles (5 km) deep. The poles are also cold because snow and ice reflects most of the little sunlight that they receive.

IN THE WIND
Water evaporates off seas and forms clouds, which, pushed by wind, travel inland and distribute water to the surface. Water vapor also transports vast quantities of energy around the Earth's atmosphere.

CRUMPLED CRUST
The Earth's mountain chains (the Alaska Range is shown above), are driven upward by collisions between adjacent crustal plates. Around the

In this satellite image of the east coast of Oman, the sea is dominant. If humans had arrived from space as colonists, "Ocean" would be a far better name for the planet than Earth.

EARTH'S INTERIOR

The Earth beneath our feet may seem steady enough, but anyone who has witnessed an erupting volcano or experienced an earthquake will know that our planet's restless interior harbors violent and destructive forces. Beneath the thin shell that we call the crust, the Earth is a seething mass of molten rock. And recent discoveries have led scientists to now believe that around the Earth's core there may be ever-shifting continents and oceans like those that exist on the surface.

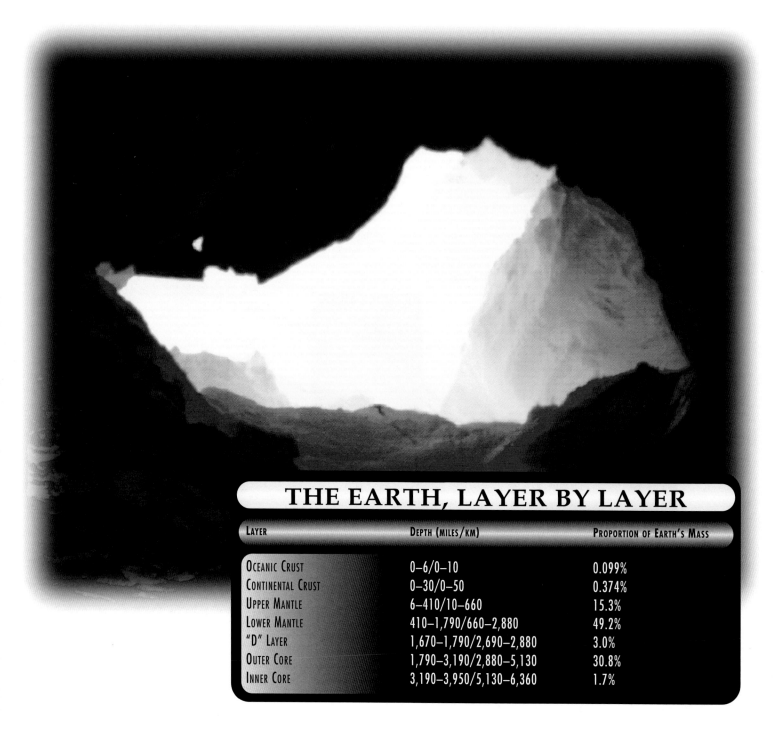

THE EARTH, LAYER BY LAYER

LAYER	DEPTH (MILES/KM)	PROPORTION OF EARTH'S MASS
OCEANIC CRUST	0–6/0–10	0.099%
CONTINENTAL CRUST	0–30/0–50	0.374%
UPPER MANTLE	6–410/10–660	15.3%
LOWER MANTLE	410–1,790/660–2,880	49.2%
"D" LAYER	1,670–1,790/2,690–2,880	3.0%
OUTER CORE	1,790–3,190/2,880–5,130	30.8%
INNER CORE	3,190–3,950/5,130–6,360	1.7%

GOING DEEP

Most people think of the Earth as a solid ball of rock, as if what lies below the soil continued all the way to the center. In fact, our planet is more like a soft-boiled egg. The outside is a thin, hard shell of rock called the crust. Immediately below it, no more than 30 miles (50 km) down, is the mantle, where the rock is hot and soft. Far beneath the mantle, some 1,860 miles (2,990 km) down, is a core of metal. In the outer part of this core the metal is molten, since it is heated by natural radioactivity to temperatures approaching those of the Sun's surface. The enormous pressure at the very center of the Earth keeps the inner core solid.

Much of what lies deep within the Earth remains a mystery, for the simple reason that it is impossible to see it. Mining and drilling barely penetrate even a quarter of the way through the crust, and we may never be able to cope with the enormous pressures and temperatures in the regions beyond even if they did.

Instead, we have to rely on indirect evidence. Much of the interplanetary debris in our part of the solar system was formed from the same material as the Earth.

When this debris falls to Earth in the form of meteorites, it yields important clues about the interior of the planet. Geoscientists also delve deep into the ocean to analyze the molten rock that is forced up from the mantle at mid-ocean ridges. Mantle minerals such as olivine often come to the surface in this way.

SHOCK TACTICS

Ironically, most of our knowledge about the Earth's interior has come from studying the seismic shock waves that accompany earthquakes. Seismic waves travel at different speeds through different rocks—for example, they travel much faster through the cold, hard rocks of the continental crust than they do through the softer, warmer rocks of the oceanic crust. So by measuring the speed of these shock waves, scientists can build up directional patterns of the rock formations below.

The most extraordinary discoveries of recent years have come from probing even farther down, to the mysterious zone of transition between the mantle and the core known as the "D" layer—short for "D double prime." As the solid minerals of the mantle give way to the molten iron and nickel of the outer core, there is an astonishing leap in density—one even greater than the difference between air and rock.

There are even more surprises at the bottom of the "D" layer, on the very boundary between mantle and core. Just as there are continents and ocean basins on the surface of the Earth, so there appear to be "anticontinents" on the core-mantle boundary that continue to shift and change in just the same way.

SOUNDINGS

THE 25-TON (23 T) "VIBROSEIS" TRUCK (RIGHT) PRODUCES CONTROLLED SHOCK WAVES THAT TRAVEL DEEP INTO THE EARTH. SCIENTISTS MEASURE THE FREQUENCY AND DIRECTION OF THOSE WAVES THAT RETURN TO THE SURFACE TO BUILD UP A PICTURE OF WHAT THE WAVES ENCOUNTERED DURING THEIR SUBTERRANEAN JOURNEY.

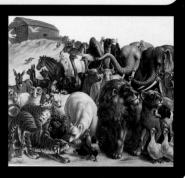

THE FLOOD

THE ENGLISH CLERIC THOMAS BURNET (1635–1715) ARGUED THAT THE EARTH CONSISTED OF WATER CONTAINED BY A SMOOTH SHELL, AND THAT THE BIBLICAL FLOOD (RIGHT) OCCURRED WHEN GOD CAUSED THIS SHELL TO CRACK. BURNET ALSO THOUGHT THAT MOUNTAINS WERE THE FRAGMENTS OF THIS SHELL. NOW IT SEEMS THAT HE WAS NOT SO FAR WRONG—EVEN THOUGH THE "FLOODING" IS BY MOLTEN ROCK, NOT WATER.

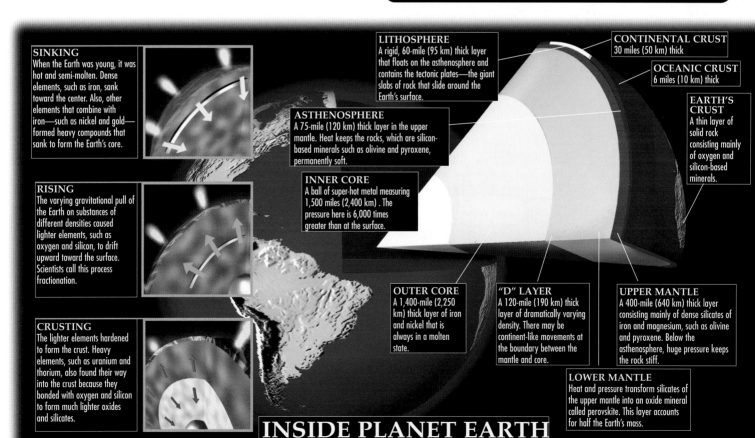

SINKING
When the Earth was young, it was hot and semi-molten. Dense elements, such as iron, sank toward the center. Also, other elements that combine with iron—such as nickel and gold—formed heavy compounds that sank to form the Earth's core.

RISING
The varying gravitational pull of the Earth on substances of different densities caused lighter elements, such as oxygen and silicon, to drift upward toward the surface. Scientists call this process fractionation.

CRUSTING
The lighter elements hardened to form the crust. Heavy elements, such as uranium and thorium, also found their way into the crust because they bonded with oxygen and silicon to form much lighter oxides and silicates.

LITHOSPHERE
A rigid, 60-mile (95 km) thick layer that floats on the asthenosphere and contains the tectonic plates—the giant slabs of rock that slide around the Earth's surface.

ASTHENOSPHERE
A 75-mile (120 km) thick layer in the upper mantle. Heat keeps the rocks, which are silicon-based minerals such as olivine and pyroxene, permanently soft.

INNER CORE
A ball of super-hot metal measuring 1,500 miles (2,400 km) . The pressure here is 6,000 times greater than at the surface.

OUTER CORE
A 1,400-mile (2,250 km) thick layer of iron and nickel that is always in a molten state.

"D" LAYER
A 120-mile (190 km) thick layer of dramatically varying density. There may be continent-like movements at the boundary between the mantle and core.

CONTINENTAL CRUST
30 miles (50 km) thick

OCEANIC CRUST
6 miles (10 km) thick

EARTH'S CRUST
A thin layer of solid rock consisting mainly of oxygen and silicon-based minerals.

UPPER MANTLE
A 400-mile (640 km) thick layer consisting mainly of dense silicates of iron and magnesium, such as olivine and pyroxene. Below the asthenosphere, huge pressure keeps the rock stiff.

LOWER MANTLE
Heat and pressure transform silicates of the upper mantle into an oxide mineral called perovskite. This layer accounts for half the Earth's mass.

INSIDE PLANET EARTH

EARTH'S IMPACT CRATERS

Every 200,000 years or so, a massive meteorite, comet, or asteroid weighing at least several hundred tons slams into Earth's surface and gouges out a huge impact crater. Scientists have identified about 150 of these "extraterrestrial impressions," ranging in size from a few hundred yards to more than 100 miles (160 km) in diameter. Many older impact craters, dating back to dinosaur times and beyond, will never be found. They have been erased from the landscape, etched away by the continuous erosion and geological activity that continues to occur on Earth.

TOP TEN IMPACT CRATERS

Location	Diameter	Age
Vredefort, Orange Free State, South Africa	187 miles (301 km)	2 billion years
Sudbury, Ontario, Canada	156 miles (251 km)	1.85 billion years
Chicxulub, Yucatan Peninsula, Mexico	125 miles (201 km)	65 million years
Manicouagan, Quebec, Canada	62 miles (100 km)	212 million years
Popigai, eastern Siberia, Russia	62 miles (100 km)	35 million years
Acraman, South Australia, Australia	56 miles (90 km)	570 million years
Puchezh-Katunki, western Russia	50 miles (80 km)	220 million years
Kara, northern Russia	40 miles (64 km)	73 million years
Beaverhead, Montana, United States	37 miles (60 km)	600 million years

SCARS FROM SPACE

Until the 1960s, most geologists believed that the craters dotted across the Earth were ancient volcanoes. Then analysis of lunar rock samples collected by Apollo astronauts proved that most of the Moon craters had been gouged out by impacts of massive debris from space. Since our atmosphere provides no defense against objects larger than about 500 feet (152 m) across, geologists were forced to conclude that the Earth must have suffered an equally severe pounding in the planet's past.

The bombardment was most intense between about 4.6 and 3.8 billion years ago, when the solar system was forming and countless rocky lumps, some the size of planets, were orbiting in a disk of swirling dust and rubble around the Sun. Since then, the storm has subsided to a "drizzle," but the threat is still there. While hundreds of tons of harmless meteorite dust fall to the Earth's surface each day, estimates suggest that a meteorite half a mile wide hits the Earth every 200,000 years on average, and an object 6 miles (10 km) in diameter collides every 50–100 million years. The last major impact event on Earth was in 1908, in sparsely populated Siberia, Russia. Luckily, there was no loss of life that time.

So where are the other impact craters? Unlike the inert Moon, the Earth is very efficient at healing impact scars. Erosion wipes out the smaller depressions within a few hundred thousand years, and even craters spanning hundreds of miles are eventually obliterated by recycling of the Earth's crust. No impact craters older than two billion years have ever been found on its surface.

Most surviving craters are either "young"—dated at a few million years old—or are located in the geologically stable continental shields of Canada, Australia, and Russia.

CRATER CREATION

While it may take millions of years to wipe away an impact crater, it only takes seconds to create one. A 60-mile (100 km) wide depression is formed in about 100 seconds. It all starts when the projectile—an asteroid or comet—hits the Earth's surface at a speed of hundreds of miles per second. At such a high velocity, crater formation is driven by shock waves generated at the point of impact. The crater is circular even if the projectile hits the surface at an oblique angle, because the shock waves automatically excavate a round hole and fling out a "curtain" of fragmented rock called ejecta that is dispersed over the surrounding terrain. The crater ends up about twenty times the diameter of the projectile.

Fragments of the projectile survive only in small craters. Bodies big enough to produce a hole more than half a mile wide are vaporized or melted by impact pressures up to 9 million times the atmospheric pressure and temperatures that may reach 8,000°F (4,430°C). But these forces inflict telltale shock damage on the rocks. Markers include deformed minerals and rock shock patterns that indicate the craters were created by forces from above. These signs can be read long after the crater landmarks have gone. In Canada, the pattern of shock effects has helped geologists map the vanished rim of Manicouagan, a 62-mile (100 km) wide crater created 212 million years ago. Clearly, the Earth's impact craters have made their mark.

DOUBLE WHAMMY
The Clearwater Lakes in Quebec, Canada, conceal a rare phenomenon—twin impact craters, thought to have been formed together by two separate but related impacts landing adjacently.

CRATER LAKE
An infrared satellite image of Elgygytgyn Lake in Siberia, Russia, shows what was once a fiery hole made by a giant meteorite. Many impact craters then fill with water, which speeds up the erosion process.

Puchezh-Katunki, western Russia

Kara, northern Russia

Beaverhead, Montana, US

Manicouagan, Quebec, Canada

Sudbury, Ontario, Canada

Popigai, eastern Siberia, Russia

The sheer size of most of the Earth's impact craters makes it hard to see them clearly from the ground.

Chicxulub, Yucatan Peninsula, Mexico

Vredefort, Orange Free State, South Africa

EARTH ATTACKED

Acraman, South Australia, Australia

SANDBLAST
Located in the Namib Desert in southern Africa, the Roter Kamm crater—the bright circle at the upper center of this space radar image—is hard to see from the ground because its floor is covered by shifting sand dunes.

STANDING PROUD
The Wolfe Creek crater in Australia is one of only a few impact craters on Earth that is well-preserved and prominently visible from the ground. The arid local environment slows down the weathering of rocks.

EARTH'S TIDES

Gravity, the force that binds the universe, is also the key to the Earth's rising and falling tides. The combined gravitational effects of the Sun and Moon constantly pull the world's oceans in different directions and create tidal effects. But there are many other factors that complicate this basic process. Friction, the Earth's spin, the tilt of its axis, and the waning power of the Moon's attraction on the far side of the Earth all conspire to make our planet's oceans a complex battleground of forces.

US TIDAL VARIATIONS

	CITY	MAXIMUM TIDAL VARIATION
1	SEATTLE, WASHINGTON	14.9 FT/4.5 M
2	CRESCENT CITY, CALIFORNIA	10.2 FT/3.1 M
3	SAN DIEGO, CALIFORNIA	8.9 FT/2.7 M
4	GALVESTON, TEXAS	2.4 FT/0.7 M
5	MOBILE, ALABAMA	2.3 FT/0.7 M
6	CHARLESTON, SOUTH CAROLINA	8.0 FT/2.4 M
7	WASHINGTON, DC	4.1 FT/1.2 M
8	NEW YORK, NEW YORK	7.0 FT/2.1 M
9	BOSTON, MASSACHUSETTS	14.7 FT/4.5 M
10	PORTLAND, MAINE	13.5 FT/4.1 M

MAKING WAVES

The water of the oceans is bound to our planet by the force of the Earth's gravity. But the Earth is not alone in space, and both the Moon and the Sun throw their own gravitational pulls into the equation. The combined effect is to tug the oceans this way and that around the globe.

The Moon's gravity stretches the Earth into an oval. The effect is so tiny that the land masses of the planet are distorted by little more than 8 inches (20 cm). But because of the fluidity of water, the effect on the oceans is more noticeable. At the point on the Earth directly beneath the Moon, the ocean is tugged into a bulge of high water. At the same time, a second tidal bulge forms on the opposite side of the planet. This is partly a result of the centrifugal force created by the Moon and Earth's combined rotation around their common center of mass, a theoretical point called the barycenter.

Because the Earth spins on its axis once every 24 hours, the two bulges sweep around the planet in waves, creating two high tides per day at every point on the globe. But the twice-daily cycle is complicated by the fact that the Earth is tilted, which puts the Moon alternately to the north and south of the equator. This creates slight differences between the two tides each day and adds a daily set of local variations to the twice-daily rhythm.

THE PLOT THICKENS

A further complication is added by the Sun, whose gravitational pull on the Earth also affects the tides. The tidal force of the Sun and Moon together is almost a third more than that of the Moon alone, with the Sun imposing a solar rhythm on the lunar rhythm. At the new and full moons, when the two bodies are in line, they combine to create extra-high spring tides. When the Moon is in its first and last quarters, the Sun is at right angles to it, and their gravitational pulls work against each other to create extra-low neap tides.

If the Earth were completely smooth, this would probably be the end of the story. But in reality, the tidal forces are weakened by friction between the ocean and the seabed to the point where the twice-daily tidal waves get slightly left behind the orbiting Moon. The waves are also continually disrupted by areas of land as they sweep around the Earth, creating yet more local variations.

At the same time, the Earth's continuous spinning on its axis causes the tidal waves to oscillate around the world's ocean basins like water in a bath. This means that high tides do not necessarily occur when the Moon is overhead, but when the oscillations accumulate to their greatest height. Each ocean basin is a different shape and so has its own unique pattern of oscillations. In the South Atlantic, for example, the tides oscillate from south to north and take around 12 hours to sweep from the tip of South Africa to the equator. In contrast, in the North Atlantic seas, they sweep in a counterclockwise direction.

Until recently, the sheer complexity of tidal forces acting on the Earth meant that the only way to predict tides was by years of patient study. Now, developments mean computer programs do the job—for which oceanographers are extremely grateful.

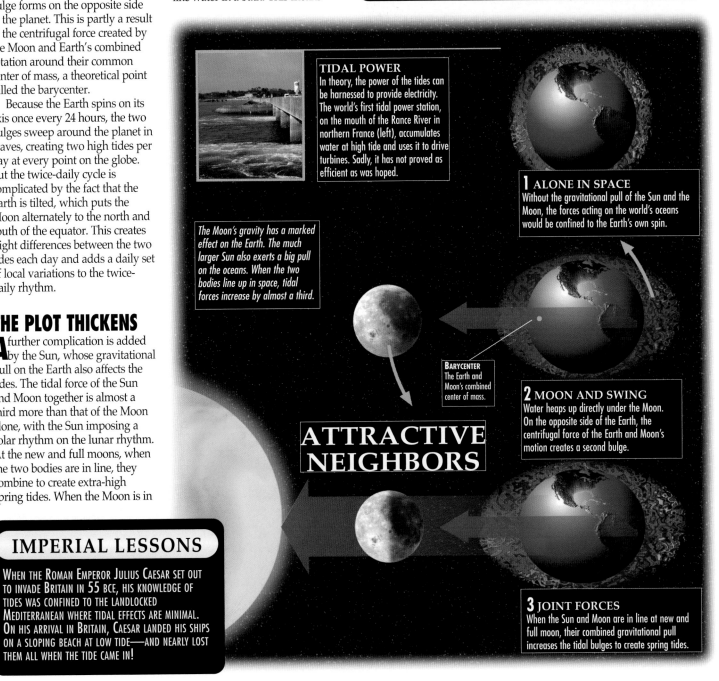

TIDAL POWER
In theory, the power of the tides can be harnessed to provide electricity. The world's first tidal power station, on the mouth of the Rance River in northern France (left), accumulates water at high tide and uses it to drive turbines. Sadly, it has not proved as efficient as was hoped.

The Moon's gravity has a marked effect on the Earth. The much larger Sun also exerts a big pull on the oceans. When the two bodies line up in space, tidal forces increase by almost a third.

1 ALONE IN SPACE
Without the gravitational pull of the Sun and the Moon, the forces acting on the world's oceans would be confined to the Earth's own spin.

BARYCENTER
The Earth and Moon's combined center of mass.

ATTRACTIVE NEIGHBORS

2 MOON AND SWING
Water heaps up directly under the Moon. On the opposite side of the Earth, the centrifugal force of the Earth and Moon's motion creates a second bulge.

3 JOINT FORCES
When the Sun and Moon are in line at new and full moon, their combined gravitational pull increases the tidal bulges to create spring tides.

IMPERIAL LESSONS

WHEN THE ROMAN EMPEROR JULIUS CAESAR SET OUT TO INVADE BRITAIN IN 55 BCE, HIS KNOWLEDGE OF TIDES WAS CONFINED TO THE LANDLOCKED MEDITERRANEAN WHERE TIDAL EFFECTS ARE MINIMAL. ON HIS ARRIVAL IN BRITAIN, CAESAR LANDED HIS SHIPS ON A SLOPING BEACH AT LOW TIDE—AND NEARLY LOST THEM ALL WHEN THE TIDE CAME IN!

THE AURORAE

The "northern lights" of the aurora borealis are among nature's most beautiful sights. With shimmering curtains of colors, dazzling white streamers, and bright green rays flashing with red, the aurorae regularly stage spectacular displays in the polar skies. For centuries, the cause of this apparently supernatural light show remained a mystery. Only recently have we come to realize that they are created by high-energy particles that stream from the Sun and collide with the Earth's atmosphere.

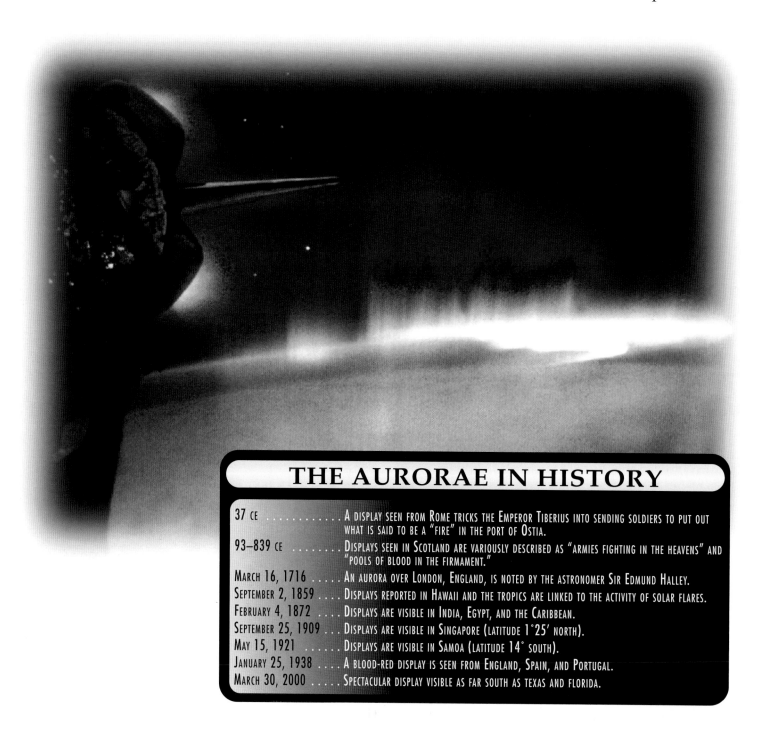

THE AURORAE IN HISTORY

37 CE	A DISPLAY SEEN FROM ROME TRICKS THE EMPEROR TIBERIUS INTO SENDING SOLDIERS TO PUT OUT WHAT IS SAID TO BE A "FIRE" IN THE PORT OF OSTIA.
93–839 CE	DISPLAYS SEEN IN SCOTLAND ARE VARIOUSLY DESCRIBED AS "ARMIES FIGHTING IN THE HEAVENS" AND "POOLS OF BLOOD IN THE FIRMAMENT."
MARCH 16, 1716	AN AURORA OVER LONDON, ENGLAND, IS NOTED BY THE ASTRONOMER SIR EDMUND HALLEY.
SEPTEMBER 2, 1859	DISPLAYS REPORTED IN HAWAII AND THE TROPICS ARE LINKED TO THE ACTIVITY OF SOLAR FLARES.
FEBRUARY 4, 1872	DISPLAYS ARE VISIBLE IN INDIA, EGYPT, AND THE CARIBBEAN.
SEPTEMBER 25, 1909	DISPLAYS ARE VISIBLE IN SINGAPORE (LATITUDE 1°25′ NORTH).
MAY 15, 1921	DISPLAYS ARE VISIBLE IN SAMOA (LATITUDE 14° SOUTH).
JANUARY 25, 1938	A BLOOD-RED DISPLAY IS SEEN FROM ENGLAND, SPAIN, AND PORTUGAL.
MARCH 30, 2000	SPECTACULAR DISPLAY VISIBLE AS FAR SOUTH AS TEXAS AND FLORIDA.

LIGHT SHOW

The aurorae (pronounced "or-ror-ree") are not occasional freaks of nature. They are a permanent feature of the Earth's upper atmosphere. Auroral displays vary in intensity, sometimes fading to almost nothing. But they are always there.

There are aurorae in both hemispheres of the Earth—the aurora borealis around the North Pole and the aurora australis around the South Pole. On satellite pictures, they show up as oval bands that encircle the Earth's magnetic poles like giant halos. The size and shape of these halos change continuously, but never disappear completely. The aurorae are gigantic and stretch high into the atmosphere. The lowest fringes hang about 50 miles (80 km) above the ground; the upper rays extend more than 600 miles (960 km) into space—three times farther than the Space Shuttle's orbit.

An auroral display resembles a giant television. In a television, streams of electrically charged particles (electrons) from the tube are guided by a magnetic field onto the lines of the screen, causing the lines to glow. In an auroral display, charged particles from the Sun strike the atoms and molecules of the Earth's atmosphere, causing them to glow in a similar way. This stream of particles is called the solar wind. It radiates continuously from the Sun's corona at over 300 miles (480 km) per second.

Fortunately for us, most of the Earth is shielded from this hurricane of charged particles by its magnetic field, which surrounds the planet like a cocoon. But there are two holes in the magnetic field, one above each magnetic pole. It is through these holes, called the polar clefts, that the solar wind pours, giving rise to the glorious colors and shapes of the aurorae.

That's show business! If the Earth's magnetic field begins to reverse and the solar wind penetrates more of the atmosphere, the aurorae could become a regular sight in the night sky of some unlikely places.

MIXING COLORS

Aurorae appear in so many colors because each gas in the atmosphere glows a different hue when struck by solar particles. The color also varies according to both the electrical state and concentration of the gas.

For example, oxygen, when struck at low altitudes, about 60 miles (100 km) up, glows a brilliant green—the most common of auroral colors. At higher altitudes, around 200 miles (320 km), it results in the vivid red aurorae that are seen during major disturbances. Nitrogen atoms, by contrast, glow blue when electrically charged (ionized) and red when neutral. Nitrogen can also emit purple light, which happens when the atoms are struck by the ultraviolet radiation contained in sunlight.

Although aurorae are everpresent, they are also everchanging. Satellites such as the IMP-8 (Interplanetary Monitoring Platform) have monitored the solar wind. From their observations we know that aurorae are at their most spectacular when the solar wind blows fiercely enough to create magnetic storms—disturbances in Earth's magnetic field. We also know that mirror-image aurorae flare simultaneously around the North and South Poles. Yet it may still be some time before we fully understand the complex relationship between aurorae, the Sun, and the Earth's magnetic field. For now, as they have done for centuries, the "northern lights" remain a beguiling mystery.

LIGHT NAMES

THE AURORAE HAVE BEEN GIVEN VARIOUS NAMES ACROSS THE WORLD. IN SCOTLAND YOU WOULD HEAR THEM REFERRED TO AS THE "MERRY DANCERS" OR THE "HEAVENLY DANCERS." THE NAME *AURORA* ITSELF COMES FROM THE LATIN WORD MEANING "DAWN." ITS FIRST KNOWN USE WAS IN A BOOK WRITTEN IN 1649 BY THE FRENCH ASTRONOMER PIERRE GASSENDI.

THE AURORA

MAKING TRACKS
Aurorae follow the angle of the Earth's magnetic field lines. This angle varies depending on longitude.

LOW OXYGEN
When solar particles strike oxygen atoms, the atoms glow green or red. In the lower atmosphere, there is mostly a green glow because the concentration of atoms is high.

HIGH OXYGEN
In the upper atmosphere there are fewer oxygen atoms. The rate of collision between the oxygen atoms is less, so red auroral displays predominate.

BLUE NITRO
Particle collisions with nitrogen are responsible for blue, purple, and red displays, depending on whether the nitrogen atoms are charged (ionized) or not.

THE MOON

The Moon is the most familiar sight in the night sky. This is because it is the Earth's closest companion and travels with the Earth in space around the Sun. The Moon orbits the Earth at a distance of just 238,850 miles (384,392 km); yet, despite being so near, it is very different from our own planet—a gray desert, dotted with craters from ancient asteroid collisions. So far the Moon is the only body in space on which humans have landed. The recent discovery of water there has stimulated plans for an eventual return.

MOON FACTS AND FIGURES

Diameter 2,160 miles (3,480 km)

Axis tilt 6° 41' relative to its orbit

Time to orbit Earth 27.3 Earth days

Length of day 27.3 Earth days

Distance from Earth 238,850 miles (384,392 km)

Surface temperature 253°F/123°C (day) to −387°F/−197°C (night)

Surface gravity 0.17 of the Earth's

Mass 0.012 of the Earth's

Volume 0.02 of the Earth's

Density 3.34 times that of water

MOONSCAPE

Since the Moon is so close, we can see its most prominent features with the naked eye. Most obvious are the dark areas that form the familiar "man-in-the-Moon" pattern. In reality these are lowlands, formed by giant meteorites that smashed into the Moon long ago, which were then filled by dark lava. They are called maria, a Latin word meaning "seas" (singular: mare); although there has never been any water in them, that is what they looked like to early observers. Many of the maria are given fanciful names, such as Mare Tranquillitatis (Sea of Tranquillity) where Apollo 11 astronauts landed in 1969. The bright areas on the Moon are highlands.

The rugged, colorless appearance of the Moon is in stark contrast to the surface of the Earth. There is no air on the Moon, so there are no clouds to spoil our view. A look through a pair of binoculars reveals that the Moon is pitted with craters, the largest of which can engulf a fair-sized city. These, too, were formed long ago by meteorite impacts. Some of the craters are surrounded by bright streaks, called rays, which consist of crushed rock thrown out by the crater-forming impacts. Lunar craters are named after famous people, mostly astronomers. The most notable example is Tycho, in the Moon's southern hemisphere, where the formation is particularly noticeable around the time of a full Moon.

BIRTH OF THE MOON

Astronomers believe that the Moon was born about 4.6 billion years ago when the youthful Earth was hit by another body, larger than the present Moon. The colliding body shattered completely under the force of the impact, which also melted part of the Earth's outer layers. The debris from the collision then went into orbit around the Earth, where it collected together to form the Moon. The lack of air and liquid water means that there is no erosion, with the result that the Moon's surface features have remained virtually unchanged for millions of years.

Whenever we look at the Moon, we always see the same side. This is because the Moon turns on its axis in exactly the same time (27.3 days) that it takes to orbit Earth—a phenomenon known as "synchronous rotation." Until space probes orbited the Moon, no one knew what the far side looked like. The first probe to photograph the Moon's far side was Russia's *Luna 3* in October 1959; since then, it has been fully mapped. The main difference is that the far side is mostly covered with bright, crater-marked highlands, and has fewer large, dark mare areas.

WHAT IF?

...WE ESTABLISHED A MOON BASE?

The discovery of water ice at the Moon's poles has stimulated plans to set up bases using pressurized cylinders, like those used in present-day space stations. The cylinders will be covered with lunar soil to protect them from cosmic rays and meteorites.

At first, scientists will use the bases to explore the mountains, craters, and valleys of the Moon to find out more about its history. Observatories will be established to obtain a clearer view of the sky than is possible from Earth, where our atmosphere gets in the way. It will also be desirable to set up radio telescopes, to study the cosmos free of interference from radio transmissions on the Earth.

Energy to power the lunar bases will come from sunlight. Solar power will also be used to convert the water ice at the poles into hydrogen and oxygen for fuel; oxygen for breathing will be extracted from the deposits currently "locked away" as oxides in the Moon's rocks. The same rocks could be used to extend the bases. Plants for food will be grown in Moon soil, with added water and fertilizer; farm animals and fish will be kept in pressurized domes.

Eventually, we will mine the Moon for the valuable minerals that it contains. Instead of rockets, magnetic ramps called mass drivers may be used to propel containers of Moon rocks into space. The rocks will then be ferried to Earth or processed in space factories. One day it may also be possible for tourists to take vacations on the Moon, living in lunar hotels and visiting sites such as Tranquillity Base, where the first Apollo astronauts landed in 1969. Analysis of the rocks brought back by the Apollo astronauts show that they contain useful metals, such as aluminum, iron, titanium, and magnesium.

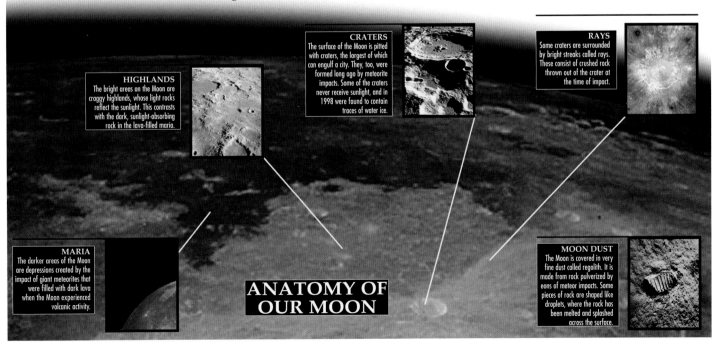

CRATERS
The surface of the Moon is pitted with craters, the largest of which can engulf a city. They, too, were formed long ago by meteorite impacts. Some of the craters never receive sunlight, and in 1998 were found to contain traces of water ice.

RAYS
Some craters are surrounded by bright streaks called rays. These consist of crushed rock thrown out of the crater at the time of impact.

HIGHLANDS
The bright areas on the Moon are craggy highlands, whose light rocks reflect the sunlight. This contrasts with the dark, sunlight-absorbing rock in the lava-filled maria.

MARIA
The darker areas of the Moon are depressions created by the impact of giant meteorites that were filled with dark lava when the Moon experienced volcanic activity.

ANATOMY OF OUR MOON

MOON DUST
The Moon is covered in very fine dust called regolith. It is made from rock pulverized by eons of meteor impacts. Some pieces of rock are shaped like droplets, where the rock has been melted and splashed across the surface.

PHASES OF
THE MOON

At one time, the phases of the Moon controlled people's lives. The full Moon made it possible to travel at night, the new Moon was thought to bring good luck, and coastal communities knew that the tides depended on the position of the Moon.

Today, few of us know what phase the Moon will be in tonight, and many people are unsure what causes its apparent changes in shape. Yet the truth is that the lunar cycle affects not only astronomers, but each and every one of us living on the Earth.

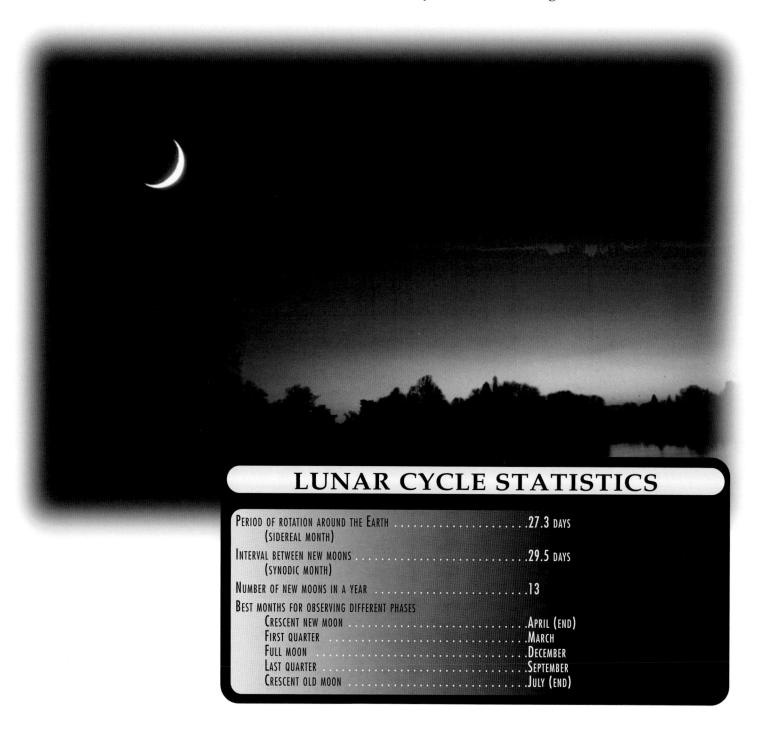

LUNAR CYCLE STATISTICS

PERIOD OF ROTATION AROUND THE EARTH (SIDEREAL MONTH)	27.3 DAYS
INTERVAL BETWEEN NEW MOONS (SYNODIC MONTH)	29.5 DAYS
NUMBER OF NEW MOONS IN A YEAR	13
BEST MONTHS FOR OBSERVING DIFFERENT PHASES	
CRESCENT NEW MOON	APRIL (END)
FIRST QUARTER	MARCH
FULL MOON	DECEMBER
LAST QUARTER	SEPTEMBER
CRESCENT OLD MOON	JULY (END)

MOONLIGHT SERENADE

The Moon's orbit around Earth is counterclockwise, like most of the orbits in our solar system. In the course of each orbit—or lunar cycle—its appearance changes from a thin crescent, through half phase to full, then back to a thin crescent again. These changes are entirely due to the angle at which the Sun's light strikes it: The Moon has no light of its own.

When the Moon is growing in size, up to full Moon, it is said to be waxing; after full, it is waning. The cycle begins at new Moon. Strictly speaking this takes place when the Moon is almost in line with the Sun, which means that it is in the daytime sky and can't normally be seen. But most people consider the Moon's first appearance as a thin crescent to be the new Moon, which occurs a day or two after the true new Moon.

The new Moon is a crescent because it is almost completely backlit. It can be seen in the western sky just after sunset, and sets soon after the Sun itself. The earliest sighting is some 14 hours after the true new Moon, but many people regard even a three- or four-day-old Moon as new. By the time the Moon is seven days old (that is, seven days after new) it has grown to a half Moon. Astronomers call this the first quarter, because the Moon is now one quarter of the way around its orbit.

WANING MOON

The half Moon can be seen more or less due south at sunset, and follows the Sun down to the west just a few hours later. After another seven days, the Moon has grown to full. Now it rises at around sunset, but is more or less directly opposite the Sun in the sky—roughly due east. The phases just before and after full Moon are called gibbous, a word which comes from the Latin *gibbosus* meaning "hunchbacked."

About a week after full, the Moon is at half phase again but with the opposite side to the first quarter illuminated. It rises roughly an hour later each night, so you will probably only see this phase early in the morning. A few days after last quarter, the Moon is back to a crescent again—this time in the predawn sky, rising an hour or two before the Sun in the east. Then, for a few days, the Moon "disappears" as it passes directly between the Earth and the Sun, signaling the start of a new cycle.

IN THE CRADLE

QUITE OFTEN WHEN THE MOON IS A CRESCENT THE WHOLE OF ITS DISK IS FAINTLY VISIBLE—SOMETIMES CALLED "THE OLD MOON IN THE NEW MOON'S ARMS." THE REASON FOR THIS PHENOMENON WOULD BE OBVIOUS IF YOU WERE STANDING ON THE MOON—ABOVE YOU WOULD BE THE NEARLY FULL EARTH WITH ITS BRILLIANT WHITE CLOUDS, CASTING LIGHT ON THE LANDSCAPE MANY TIMES BRIGHTER THAN THE FULL MOON DOES IN OUR SKY.

TRUE STORY

MANY PEOPLE OBSERVE THAT THE MOON APPEARS TO BE BIGGER WHEN IT IS RISING THAN WHEN IT IS HIGH UP IN THE SKY. BUT, IF ANYTHING, THE MOON IS SLIGHTLY SMALLER WHEN IT IS RISING. ITS APPARENT SIZE IS AN ILLUSION. THE REASON FOR THIS IS THAT YOUR EYE COMPARES THE RISING MOON WITH DISTANT OBJECTS ON THE LANDSCAPE—NOT, AS SOME BOOKS SUGGEST, THE LENSING EFFECT OF THE AIR NEAR THE HORIZON "MAGNIFYING" THE IMAGE.

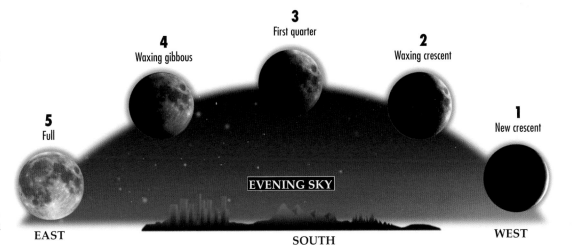

4 Waxing gibbous

3 First quarter

2 Waxing crescent

5 Full

1 New crescent

EVENING SKY

EAST

SOUTH

WEST

THE LUNAR MONTH

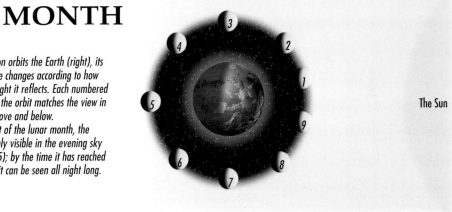

As the Moon orbits the Earth (right), its appearance changes according to how much sunlight it reflects. Each numbered position in the orbit matches the view in the sky above and below.
At the start of the lunar month, the Moon is only visible in the evening sky (views 1–5); by the time it has reached full Moon it can be seen all night long.

The Sun

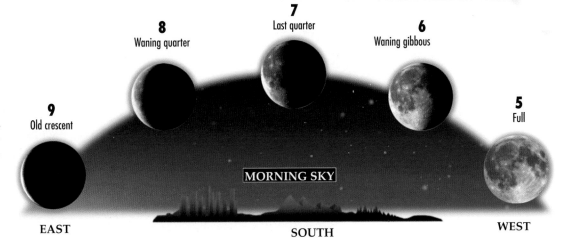

8 Waning quarter

7 Last quarter

6 Waning gibbous

9 Old crescent

5 Full

MORNING SKY

EAST

SOUTH

WEST

FORMATION
OF THE MOON

The Moon is an oddity—a satellite so large that the Earth-Moon system is almost a double planet. For generations, rival theories strove to explain its origin. But evidence brought back by the Apollo landings may have settled the argument. Most scientists now believe that 4.5 billion years ago, the molten, new-made Earth was struck a glancing blow by another planet. The impact destroyed the wanderer and hurled huge chunks of the Earth into space. From this ancient collision, our nearest neighbor was born.

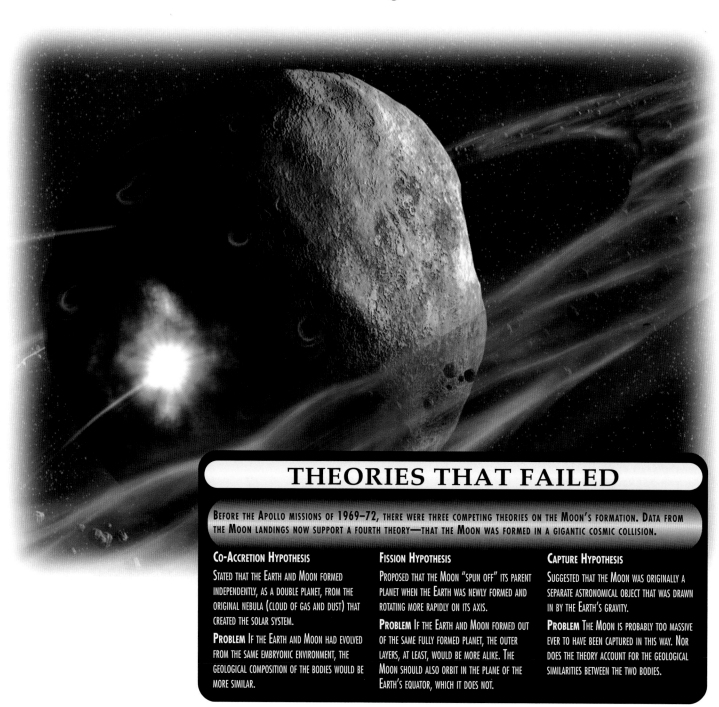

THEORIES THAT FAILED

BEFORE THE APOLLO MISSIONS OF 1969–72, THERE WERE THREE COMPETING THEORIES ON THE MOON'S FORMATION. DATA FROM THE MOON LANDINGS NOW SUPPORT A FOURTH THEORY—THAT THE MOON WAS FORMED IN A GIGANTIC COSMIC COLLISION.

CO-ACCRETION HYPOTHESIS

STATED THAT THE EARTH AND MOON FORMED INDEPENDENTLY, AS A DOUBLE PLANET, FROM THE ORIGINAL NEBULA (CLOUD OF GAS AND DUST) THAT CREATED THE SOLAR SYSTEM.

PROBLEM IF THE EARTH AND MOON HAD EVOLVED FROM THE SAME EMBRYONIC ENVIRONMENT, THE GEOLOGICAL COMPOSITION OF THE BODIES WOULD BE MORE SIMILAR.

FISSION HYPOTHESIS

PROPOSED THAT THE MOON "SPUN OFF" ITS PARENT PLANET WHEN THE EARTH WAS NEWLY FORMED AND ROTATING MORE RAPIDLY ON ITS AXIS.

PROBLEM IF THE EARTH AND MOON FORMED OUT OF THE SAME FULLY FORMED PLANET, THE OUTER LAYERS, AT LEAST, WOULD BE MORE ALIKE. THE MOON SHOULD ALSO ORBIT IN THE PLANE OF THE EARTH'S EQUATOR, WHICH IT DOES NOT.

CAPTURE HYPOTHESIS

SUGGESTED THAT THE MOON WAS ORIGINALLY A SEPARATE ASTRONOMICAL OBJECT THAT WAS DRAWN IN BY THE EARTH'S GRAVITY.

PROBLEM THE MOON IS PROBABLY TOO MASSIVE EVER TO HAVE BEEN CAPTURED IN THIS WAY. NOR DOES THE THEORY ACCOUNT FOR THE GEOLOGICAL SIMILARITIES BETWEEN THE TWO BODIES.

IMPACT
A wandering planet, traveling at several miles per second, plunges into the young Earth, still hot from its recent formation. Within four hours, the core of the impacting planet merges with the Earth's mantle and the outermost layers of both planets are blasted into space.

DEBRIS
Under the influence of the Earth's gravity and centrifugal force (the force that pulls an orbiting body away from the center of its orbit), debris from the collision swirls into a gigantic disk. Much of the material in the disk falls back to Earth, but the rest begins to coalesce into steadily larger objects.

MOONBIRTH
Within a few years, the largest bodies in the disk have swept up most of the free debris and gathered together to form a single large satellite. The Earth–Moon system is now complete, but still young and hot. In time, the two bodies will cool and drift apart to form the system that exists today.

The Moon is the fifth-largest natural satellite in the solar system. Only Pluto's moon Charon—which is nearly half Pluto's diameter—is bigger in relation to its parent planet.

COSMIC COLLISION

Astronomers may never know for sure how the Moon was formed, but most today favor the so-called "giant impact" theory. The early solar system was a chaotic place—a whirling disk of spinning debris that slowly clumped together to form the planets. The giant impact theory proposes that in the midst of this vortex, the infant Earth was hit by another planet-sized body. The catastrophic collision sent a vast cloud of debris swirling around what remained of the Earth, and this debris later coalesced to form the Moon.

The beauty of the giant impact theory is that it explains both the differences and the similarities between the two bodies. The composition of the Moon and Earth are similar, but by no means identical. Some differences can be explained by gravity—the Earth's core has more iron than the Moon's, for instance, because the Earth's greater mass would naturally have attracted the heaviest material. But some lunar rock is quite unlike any on Earth—perhaps because it came from the debris of a shattered impacting planet.

The theory evolved in the early 1970s, when data from the Apollo missions began to cast doubt over earlier ideas on how the Moon was formed. Two astronomers, William Hartmann and Donald Davis, from the Planetary Sciences Institute in Tucson, Arizona, had been estimating the sizes of miniplanets, or planetesimals, that might have formed near to the Earth in the early days of the solar system.

IMPACT SIMULATIONS

Davis and Hartmann's research showed that several objects, each much larger than the present-day Moon, could have coalesced near enough to Earth to pose an impact threat, and that such an impact would create the right quantity of debris to form a satellite just like the Moon.

At first, astronomers could only guess at the size of the impacting body needed to release such a vast amount of material. But now, with the help of computer simulations of impacts, they can follow the progress of between 1,000 and 3,000 interacting fragments that vary in size from a few dozen miles to a few hundred miles across. The simulations appear to confirm that a giant impact at a certain angle could have led to the formation of the Earth-Moon system within just a few years. And in July 1997, a team of scientists from the University of Colorado presented the latest estimate for impacting body's mass. They showed that around 60–85 percent of the debris in an orbiting disk simply falls to the surface of the parent planet. This implied that for the remainder to coalesce into a satellite the size of the present-day Moon, the Earth must have been hit by an object 2.5–3 times the size of Mars.

Even so, the giant impact theory is not conclusively proved. To date, all of the computer simulations that lead from giant impact to the formation of a Moon-sized satellite leave the Earth rotating about twice as fast as geological evidence suggests that it should have been at the time. Our nearest neighbor is not about to give up its secrets so easily—if it ever does so.

MOTHER MOON

THE IROQUOIS BELIEVE THE MOON WAS FORMED BY HAHGWEHDIYU, THE "GOOD CREATOR" (RIGHT). HE SHAPED THE SKY WITH THE PALM OF HIS HANDS, AND THEN USED HIS DEAD MOTHER'S BODY AS RAW MATERIAL TO MAKE THE SUN, THE MOON, AND THE STARS.

REFORMED?

MIRANDA, ONE OF THE SATELLITES OF URANUS, WAS ONCE THOUGHT TO HAVE A HISTORY AS VIOLENT AS THE MOON'S. MIRANDA'S TERRAIN INCLUDES THREE RELATIVELY YOUNG AND HEAVILY RIDGED AREAS, WHILE THE REST OF THE LANDSCAPE IS OLDER AND CRATERED, IMPLYING THAT IT REFORMED AFTER BEING SHATTERED IN A GIANT IMPACT. BUT NOWADAYS MOST ASTRONOMERS THINK THAT THE GIANT RIDGES ARE DUE TO TIDAL VOLCANIC ACTIVITY OF THE TYPE THAT ALSO FLEXES JUPITER'S MOON IO.

MARS

Mars is the fourth planet from the Sun and one of Earth's nearest neighbors. It is also the only other planet in the solar system where humans may one day live. Mars is smaller and colder than Earth, but is otherwise remarkably similar. It has days and seasons, a thin atmosphere, and, probably, significant reserves of water buried as ice beneath the surface. There is even a chance that Mars once played host to simple life-forms, and that the fossilized remains of long-extinct creatures are still buried there.

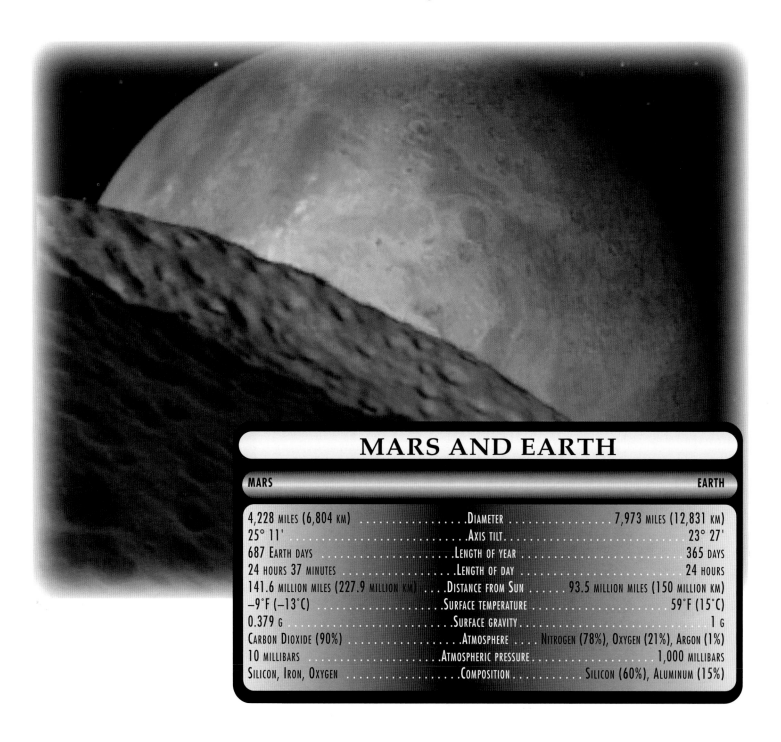

MARS AND EARTH

MARS		EARTH
4,228 miles (6,804 km)	Diameter	7,973 miles (12,831 km)
25° 11'	Axis tilt	23° 27'
687 Earth days	Length of year	365 days
24 hours 37 minutes	Length of day	24 hours
141.6 million miles (227.9 million km)	Distance from Sun	93.5 million miles (150 million km)
−9°F (−13°C)	Surface temperature	59°F (15°C)
0.379 g	Surface gravity	1 g
Carbon Dioxide (90%)	Atmosphere	Nitrogen (78%), Oxygen (21%), Argon (1%)
10 millibars	Atmospheric pressure	1,000 millibars
Silicon, Iron, Oxygen	Composition	Silicon (60%), Aluminum (15%)

A COLD, ROCKY DESERT

Of all the planets in the solar system, Mars is the most like ours. Its axis is tilted like the Earth's, which gives it seasons. Mars has a relatively warm summer, when temperatures in the southern hemisphere can reach up to 68°F (20°C), but a long, cold winter that sees them plunge to –284°F (–140°C).

Over 4 billion years ago, Mars was covered with massive volcanoes—just like the Earth— and had surface water, which occasionally gathered in flash floods, carving water channels into the surface. There may even have been standing oceans over long periods of time. Like the Earth, too, Mars has a cloudy atmosphere; although the Martian "air" is much thinner, and the wispy clouds are made of carbon dioxide rather than water vapor.

So, despite its many similarities to Earth, Mars is a far from hospitable place. If you landed there without a spacesuit, not only would you suffocate but, due to the much lower atmospheric pressure, your blood would boil within minutes.

DUST STORMS

Apart from the lack of oxygen and the low atmospheric pressure, you would also have to withstand the continuous winds that blow across the Martian surface at speeds of over 125 miles per hour (200 kmh), whipping up giant clouds of fine orange-brown dust in their wake. It is this dust that has earned Mars the nickname "The Red Planet," although "Rusty Planet" might be more suitable, since the color is explained by the high proportion of iron in the planet's rocks—on average, this measures almost twice as much as on Earth. Mars is also very dry and cold. Even on a warm summer's day the ground rarely gets above freezing point, and on winter mornings the rocks

are often coated with a fine layer of carbon dioxide "frost."

Mars's two moons, Phobos and Deimos, race around the planet in about eight hours and 30 hours respectively. They are thought to be asteroids that strayed too close to the planet in the distant past and were captured by its gravity. If Phobos, the closer of the two, maintains its present orbit, it is likely to crash into Mars in about 100,000 years' time. Some evidence even suggests Mars has suffered similar collisions in the past.

NATURAL FEATURES

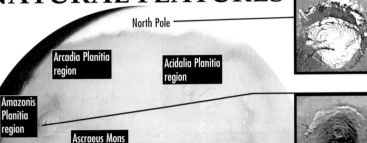

North Pole

Arcadia Planitia region

Acidalia Planitia region

Amazonis Planitia region

Ascraeus Mons

Mangala Vallis

Pavonis Mons

Valles Marineris region

Arsia Mons

Noctis Labyrinthus

Magaritifer Sinus region

South Pole

When the first truly detailed maps of Mars were made in the 1970s, scientists added descriptive Latin words such as Planitia ("plain") or Mons ("mountain") to the original place names.

NORTH POLE
Made of frozen carbon dioxide (dry ice) and water ice. The southern ice cap shrinks away to almost nothing in the summer.

OLYMPUS MONS
The largest volcano in the solar system, it stretches 17 miles (27 km) high and is 375 miles (600 km) across. It is probably extinct.

VALLES MARINERIS CANYON
A giant canyon across one side of Mars, 3,125 miles (5,030 km) long and big enough for the Rocky Mountains to fit comfortably inside.

ARGYRE PLANITIA
One of many basins on Mars created long ago by asteroid impacts. The crater Galle is about 125 miles (200 km) across.

CANAL MYTH

THE BIGGEST MYTH ABOUT MARS—THAT A RACE OF MARTIANS ONCE BUILT CANALS TO CARRY WATER FROM THE POLES TO THE EQUATOR—IS BASED ON A TRANSLATION ERROR. IN 1877, THE ITALIAN ASTRONOMER GIOVANNI SCHIAPARELLI SAW WHAT HE THOUGHT WERE "CANALI," MEANING "CHANNELS," THROUGH HIS TELESCOPE. IN ENGLISH THIS WAS TRANSLATED AS "CANALS" SO PEOPLE ASSUMED THEY MUST BE ARTIFICIAL WATERWAYS. IN FACT, THEY WERE AN OPTICAL ILLUSION.

LIVE FROM MARS
On July 4, 1997, the uncrewed US probe *Pathfinder* became the first spacecraft to land on Mars since *Viking* in 1976. After a short delay due to technical glitches, *Pathfinder* released the *Sojourner* remote-controlled Mars rover, and the world held its breath as the probe's first pictures were broadcast back to Earth.

THE SURFACE OF MARS

Rust staining in the soil, imparted by iron oxide, is the simple reason why Mars's surface is so distinctly red. But its color is just one of the planet's unique surface features. In recent years, the Martian surface has been revealed as a rich and varied landscape, shaped by great natural forces such as meteorite impacts, floods, volcanoes, earthquakes, and glaciers. Mars's surface is continuing to evolve, due to seasonal freezing and thawing and powerful winds that transport vast clouds of dust across its face.

TOP TEN SURFACE FEATURES

NAME OF FEATURE	TYPE OF FEATURE	LOCATION	SIZE MILES/KM
VALLES MARINERIS	Tectonic canyon system	70°W, 10°S	2,500 miles (4,023 km) long, 373 miles (600 km) at its widest, and 5 miles (8 km) deep
THARSIS RIDGE	Basalt plateau	100°W, 5°N	6 miles (10 km) high by 2,485 miles (4,000 km) wide
OLYMPUS MONS	Extinct shield volcano	135°W, 20°N	17 miles (27 km) high by 373 miles (600 km) wide (largest volcano known)
SYRTIS MAJOR PLANITIA	Dark, elevated flat plain	290°E, 10°N	785 miles (1,265 km) in diameter
NORTH POLE ICE CAP	Frozen H_2O and CO_2	Extends to 65°N in winter	Maximum thickness of 3 miles (5 km); 1,000 miles (1,600 km) wide in winter, 375 miles (600 km) wide in summer
SOUTH POLE	Composed mainly of CO_2	Extends to 45°S in winter	1,200 miles (1,930 km) wide in winter, 250 miles (400 km) wide in summer
ARGYRE PLANITIA	Impact basin	42°W, 50°S	870 miles (1,400 km) in diameter
ACIDALIA PLANITIA	Impact basin	30°E, 50°N	1,625 miles (2,615 km) in diameter
HELLAS BASIN	Impact basin	294°E, 40°S	1,000 by 1,250 miles (1,600 by 2010 km) (Mars's largest impact crater)
ELYSIUM PLANITIA	Impact basin	210°E, 20°N	1,554 miles (2,500 km) in diameter

ROCKS OF AGES

We know a great deal about the Martian surface, thanks first to nineteenth-century astronomers, who identified and named many of its features, and more recently to uncrewed Mars probes that have provided us with stunning closeups of the entire planet.

Much of the surface of Mars is a barren stony desert that looks and behaves much like deserts on Earth. But Mars has a range of distinctive features. Most of them, such as mountains, canyons, extinct volcanoes, and craters, were created early in the planet's life. Mars's rivers, and probably its seas, have since shaped and modified many of these landmarks. Some of Mars's most unusual features—like the "Main Pyramid," "City Square," and "The Face"—have even led to claims that they might be ruins left by an ancient civilization, although most scientists now believe they are natural features.

But the planet's reddish soil can be found everywhere on Mars—the result of billions of years of rock erosion by wind and water and pulverization by meteorites. This soil, blown around by the wind, covers virtually the entire planet and can be a few inches or many feet deep. It collects to forms drifts, which can be seen from high above the planet's surface as distinctive tapered streaks of soil, often deposited on the leeward sides of Mars's craters.

Most of what is known about the composition of Martian soil comes from experiments performed by the Viking landers. They detected iron-rich clays, calcium carbonate, iron oxides, and magnesium sulfate, as well as silicon dioxide, which makes up 50 percent of Mars's soil. The strange oxidizing agent in the soil, which releases oxygen when wetted, is thought to be a type of peroxide.

The Martian surface can be split into two regions. The highlands, in the southern hemisphere, contain Mars's oldest surface rocks. Many craters, some more than 50 miles (80 km) wide, and basins are found here. The lowlands, in the northern hemisphere, are less cratered. This is the flattest, smoothest region known in the solar system. Some scientists believe it was shaped by ancient ocean water, as it resembles the heavily sedimented floors of Earth's oceans. Mars's largest volcanoes also exist in the lowlands in an area known as Tharsis Ridge.

Next to Tharsis Ridge, in the equatorial region, lies the Valles Marineris, a canyon stretching almost the distance from New York to California. But unlike the Earth's Grand Canyon, which was cut by the Colorado River, the Valles Marineris canyon is thought to be an ancient tectonic feature, caused by movement in Mars's surface mantle. Other features found here are channels, probably cut by frequent flooding more than a billion years ago, and large sand dunes.

More impressive sand dunes surround each of the poles. A big dune field entirely circles the northern pole, showing just how important the strong Martian wind is in the carving and shaping of this unique landscape.

CLOSE CALL

THE VIKING LANDERS HAD TO TOUCH DOWN ON EVEN GROUND FOR THEIR EXPERIMENTS TO SUCCEED. *VIKING 1* LANDED ON AN AREA THAT LOOKED LIKE A SMOOTH, SPARSELY CRATERED PLAIN—FROM ORBIT. BUT IT HAD COME WITHIN 30 FEET (9 M) OF CATASTROPHE IN THE SHAPE OF A 7-FOOT (2 M) WIDE ROCK, LATER NAMED BIG JOE (RIGHT). *VIKING 2* LANDED NEAR SEVERAL CHANNELS. BUT BOTH MADE IT, DESPITE THESE UNSEEN OBSTRUCTIONS.

ROMANTIC

MARS WAS FIRST SEEN BY GALILEO IN 1610, BUT IT WAS NOT UNTIL 1867 THAT ASTRONOMER RICHARD PROCTOR SYSTEMATICALLY NAMED MARS'S FEATURES AFTER SCIENTISTS WHO HAD STUDIED THE PLANET. TEN YEARS LATER, ITALIAN ASTRONOMER GIOVANNI SCHIAPARELLI (PICTURED) REFASHIONED MARS ROMANTICALLY, CREATING EVOCATIVE NEW NAMES SUCH AS MARE SIRENUM (SEA OF SIRENS) AND ELYSIUM PLANITIA (DELIGHTFUL PLAINS), BASED ON CLASSICAL LITERATURE AND THE BIBLE. ARABIA, EDEN, THARSIS, AND ELYSIUM.

TWO FACES OF MARS

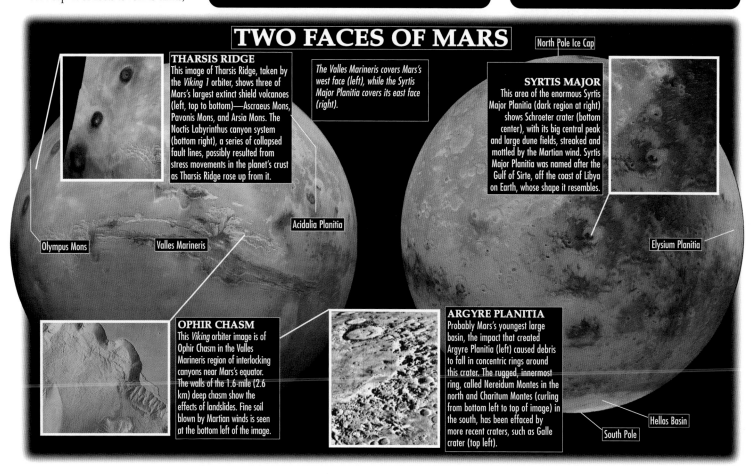

North Pole Ice Cap

THARSIS RIDGE
This image of Tharsis Ridge, taken by the *Viking 1* orbiter, shows three of Mars's largest extinct shield volcanoes (left, top to bottom)—Ascraeus Mons, Pavonis Mons, and Arsia Mons. The Noctis Labyrinthus canyon system (bottom right), a series of collapsed fault lines, possibly resulted from stress movements in the planet's crust as Tharsis Ridge rose up from it.

The Valles Marineris covers Mars's west face (left), while the Syrtis Major Planitia covers its east face (right).

SYRTIS MAJOR
This area of the enormous Syrtis Major Planitia (dark region at right) shows Schroeter crater (bottom center), with its big central peak and large dune fields, streaked and mottled by the Martian wind. Syrtis Major Planitia was named after the Gulf of Sirte, off the coast of Libya on Earth, whose shape it resembles.

Acidalia Planitia

Olympus Mons

Valles Marineris

Elysium Planitia

OPHIR CHASM
This *Viking* orbiter image is of Ophir Chasm in the Valles Marineris region of interlocking canyons near Mars's equator. The walls of the 1.6-mile (2.6 km) deep chasm show the effects of landslides. Fine soil blown by Martian winds is seen at the bottom left of the image.

ARGYRE PLANITIA
Probably Mars's youngest large basin, the impact that created Argyre Planitia (left) caused debris to fall in concentric rings around this crater. The rugged, innermost ring, called Nereidum Montes in the north and Charitum Montes (curling from bottom left to top of image) in the south, has been effaced by more recent craters, such as Galle crater (top left).

Hellas Basin

South Pole

WATER ON MARS

The Italian astronomer Giovanni Schiaparelli (1835–1910) started a myth when he said he'd seen canali (channels) on Mars. These were later found to be an optical illusion as well as a scientific impossibility—spectroscopic analysis of light from Mars showed a dry place with so little atmosphere that water would have boiled away instantly. Yet Mars wasn't always a desert. Space probes have discovered the remains of dried-up riverbeds, channels carved by water, flood plains, and shallow seas, so what happened in the distant past to freeze-dry the entire planet?

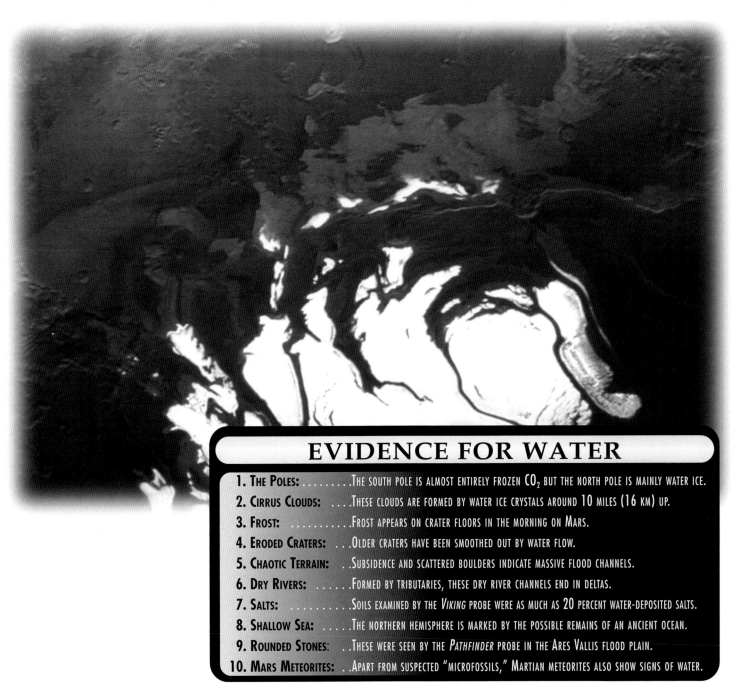

EVIDENCE FOR WATER

1. **The Poles:** . . . . The south pole is almost entirely frozen CO_2 but the north pole is mainly water ice.

2. **Cirrus Clouds:** . . . .These clouds are formed by water ice crystals around 10 miles (16 km) up.

3. **Frost:** . . . . .Frost appears on crater floors in the morning on Mars.

4. **Eroded Craters:** . . .Older craters have been smoothed out by water flow.

5. **Chaotic Terrain:** . .Subsidence and scattered boulders indicate massive flood channels.

6. **Dry Rivers:** . . . . . .Formed by tributaries, these dry river channels end in deltas.

7. **Salts:** . . . . .Soils examined by the *Viking* probe were as much as 20 percent water-deposited salts.

8. **Shallow Sea:** . . . . .The northern hemisphere is marked by the possible remains of an ancient ocean.

9. **Rounded Stones:** . .These were seen by the *Pathfinder* probe in the Ares Vallis flood plain.

10. **Mars Meteorites:** . .Apart from suspected "microfossils," Martian meteorites also show signs of water.

FROZEN IN TIME

Planetary scientists were slow to discover Mars's secret history. The first probes to fly past the Red Planet returned only a handful of images, which showed Moon-like cratered plains. And when *Mariner 9* orbited Mars in 1971, it took many months for the spacecraft to begin mapping the planet—almost all of Mars's features were obscured by a global dust storm. But when the storm eventually cleared, *Mariner 9's* pictures proved to be worth the wait. They showed enormous volcanoes, far bigger than any found on Earth. They also showed a multitude of features that suggested liquid water had once scoured the planet's surface. These included vast canyons, eroded craters, chaotic terrain of broken rock caused by sudden flooding, and long, riverlike channels fed by tributaries that run downhill.

Although some researchers tried to dismiss this evidence, suggesting other processes such as lava flows that might have caused erosion, successive spacecraft have only strengthened the evidence for a once-watery Mars. Orbiter spacecraft such as the *Vikings*, *Mars Global Surveyor*, and *Mars Express* have provided ever-clearer images of water-formed features, while Mars rovers—in particular *Spirit* and *Curiosity*, which landed in 2012—have discovered minerals in the Martian soil that could only have formed if the surface was submerged for sustained periods of time. Astronomers still argue over the extent of the water, though—some imagine short-lived temporary lakes on the surface, but others suggest Mars was once a blue planet, with a great ocean, the Oceanus Borealis.

Another question is when and how the water disappeared. One suggestion is that radiation from the Sun was able to break up water molecules in the atmosphere, and because of the weak gravity, light hydrogen atoms were then carried away by the solar wind. Another idea is that the water remains in underground reservoirs. In 2002, the Mars *Odyssey* probe detected the signature from massive amounts of water ice just below the surface around both the north and south poles.

On Earth, the geological process of plate tectonics recycles carbonates from rocks into the air, as continental plate movements redistribute the molten mantle. Mars lacked the energy for this process. If carbon and oxygen from the air got chemically locked into the Martian rocks, they stayed there—shrinking the atmosphere further. In a reverse greenhouse effect, the thinner the atmosphere got, the colder it became. Perhaps two billion years ago, much of the remaining atmosphere became frozen carbon dioxide—or dry ice—and the last of the water retreated below the surface, finding refuge at the planet's poles.

DELTA GROOVES

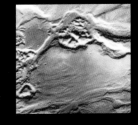

THE *MARINER 9* SPACECRAFT BROUGHT BACK THE FIRST PICTURES OF MANGALA VALLIS—A 370-MILE (595 KM), WATER-CARVED OUTFLOW CHANNEL RUNNING ACROSS MARS'S SOUTHERN HEMISPHERE. THE CHANNEL IS PROBABLY THE PRODUCT OF MASSIVE FLOODING BY WATER THAT BROKE THROUGH FROM BENEATH THE PLANET'S SURFACE CRUST. JUST LIKE A RIVER ON EARTH, IT BEGINS WITH A NETWORK OF TRIBUTARIES, WHICH THEN MEET IN A NARROW MAIN CHANNEL. THIS RUNS DOWNHILL, EVENTUALLY THICKENING OUT AT THE MOUTH (SEE ABOVE) LIKE A TERRESTRIAL RIVER DELTA. STRUCK BY ITS SIMILARITY IN SIZE AND SHAPE TO THE GREATEST RIVER ON EARTH, SCIENTISTS DECIDED TO NAME ITS DOWNSTREAM PLAIN AMAZONIS PLANITIA.

LAYERED ROCK
This image from the *Mars Global Surveyor* spacecraft shows layered rock in the Coprates Catena area, which lies at the center of the massive Valles Marineris canyon. Layered rock on Earth, such as that found in Arizona's Grand Canyon, is often the result of sediment deposited by ancient lakes.

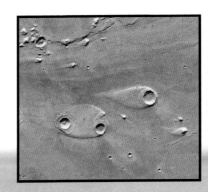

ISLANDS
The water that carved channels to the north and east of the vast Valles Marineris canyon had huge erosive power. One consequence was the formation of streamlined islands where the water encountered obstacles. This image shows islands formed as the water was diverted by large craters in its path.

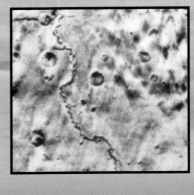

TRIBUTARIES
This *Viking* image of the Nirgil Vallis canyon shows tributaries off the main channel. They were probably formed by springs located on cliffs overlooking the canyon. As the water weakened the cliffs, they eventually collapsed. Each collapse forged a new tributary, which grew longer as the spring maintained it.

JUPITER

The fifth planet from the Sun, the mighty Jupiter is by far the largest in the solar system. Over 1,300 Earths could fit inside it, and it is more than twice as massive as all the other planets put together. Jupiter has a complex weather system, which generates the bands of clouds that swirl across its surface and also includes the planet's best-known feature, the Great Red Spot—itself up to three times the size of Earth. Like its neighbors in the outer solar system, Jupiter has rings. It also has at least sixty-three moons, which have been likened to a miniature solar system.

JUPITER PROFILE

JUPITER		EARTH
88,846 miles (142,983 km)	Diameter	7,973 miles (12,831 km)
3° 10′	Axis Tilt	23° 27′
4,329 days (11.86 Earth years)	Length of Year	365 days
9 hours 55 minutes 29 seconds	Length of Day	24 hours
483.7 million miles (778.4 million km)	Distance from Sun	93.5 million miles (150 million km)
−186°F (−85°C)	Surface Temperature	59°F (15°C)
2.53 g	Surface Gravity	1 g
Hydrogen (90%), Helium (10%), Methane (0.07%)	Atmosphere	Nitrogen (79%), Oxygen (21%)
700 millibars	Atmospheric Pressure	1,000 millibars
Hydrogen (90%), Helium (10%), Methane (0.07%)	Composition	Silicon (60%), Aluminum (15%)

GIANT PLANET

Like the other gas giants of the solar system—Saturn, Uranus, and Neptune—Jupiter has no solid surface. The planet has a rocky core, but most of it consists of gases that become more and more dense toward the center until they eventually turn to liquid. The striking patterns observed by space probes and telescopes are not surface features but clouds. Their bands, swirls, and eddies are the outward signs of the immensely powerful weather engine that drives Jupiter's atmosphere.

The clouds have arranged themselves into nineteen clearly defined bands in shades of red, amber, and brown. The winds in adjacent bands blow in opposite directions at speeds of 250 miles per hour (400 kmh) or more. The cloud bands are probably the outer surfaces of thick layers of atmospheric material that rotate around the planet and extend deep into its interior. The bands themselves are remarkably stable. Although the cloud patterns within them are constantly changing, there are features in

Jupiter's cloudscapes that have been there for many years, or even centuries. The best-known of them is the aptly named Great Red Spot, a vast anticyclonic storm up to three times the size of the Earth that has existed for at least three hundred years.

Jupiter's atmosphere is about 5,000 miles (8,050 km) thick and consists mostly of hydrogen. There is also some helium and small quantities of methane and ammonia, plus traces of other compounds. Beneath these gases

is an ocean of hot liquid hydrogen. Even at more than 3,150°F (1,732°C), the hydrogen does not boil away. It is kept under a pressure that measures some 90,000 times that of the atmosphere on Earth.

Jupiter's liquid hydrogen layer is over 30,000 miles (48,280 km) thick. Far beneath it, under what scientists believe may be a layer of water and ammonia, is a rocky core measuring around 4,200 miles (6,760 km) across.

Deep within the planet, the pressure reaches 45 million Earth atmospheres and temperatures rise to more than 20,000°F (11,000°C). Under these extreme conditions, the liquid hydrogen takes on some of the characteristics of a metal. Electric currents flow through it and generate Jupiter's magnetic field, which, after the Sun's, is the strongest in the solar system.

KINGS OF GODS

JUPITER IS NAMED FOR THE KING OF THE ROMAN GODS, WHO IS USUALLY DEPICTED HURLING A THUNDERBOLT. HE WAS ALSO KNOWN AS JOVE AND, TO THE ANCIENT GREEKS, AS ZEUS. THE PLANET'S MOONS ARE NAMED FOR OTHER CHARACTERS IN THE GREEK MYTHS OF ZEUS, MOST OF THEM HIS LOVERS.

BETHLEHEM'S STAR?

THE STAR OF BETHLEHEM MAY HAVE BEEN THE CONJUNCTION (COMING TOGETHER) IN THE SKY OF JUPITER AND ONE OR MORE OF THE OTHER BRIGHT PLANETS. SEVERAL CONJUNCTIONS OCCURRED AROUND THE TIME THE "STAR" IS SAID TO HAVE APPEARED.

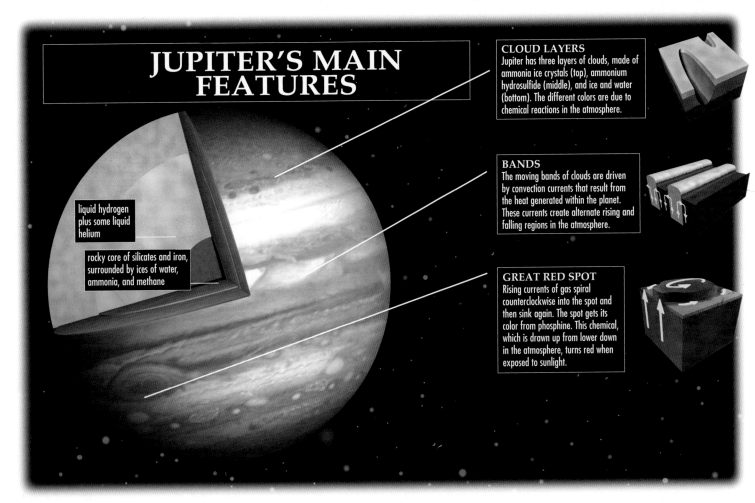

JUPITER'S MAIN FEATURES

CLOUD LAYERS
Jupiter has three layers of clouds, made of ammonia ice crystals (top), ammonium hydrosulfide (middle), and ice and water (bottom). The different colors are due to chemical reactions in the atmosphere.

BANDS
The moving bands of clouds are driven by convection currents that result from the heat generated within the planet. These currents create alternate rising and falling regions in the atmosphere.

GREAT RED SPOT
Rising currents of gas spiral counterclockwise into the spot and then sink again. The spot gets its color from phosphine. This chemical, which is drawn up from lower down in the atmosphere, turns red when exposed to sunlight.

liquid hydrogen plus some liquid helium

rocky core of silicates and iron, surrounded by ices of water, ammonia, and methane

JUPITER'S ATMOSPHERE

Jupiter is the largest planet in the solar system—bigger than all the others put together—and its weather is on a scale to match. Turbulent winds, fierce lightning, and raging storms keep the atmosphere constantly churning. Three multicolored cloud layers wrap the entire globe in ever-changing, swirling patterns, rotating in bands that move either with or against the planet's spin. The *Voyager* and *Galileo* probes have sent back vivid pictures and valuable data that reveal the complexity of Jupiter's atmosphere.

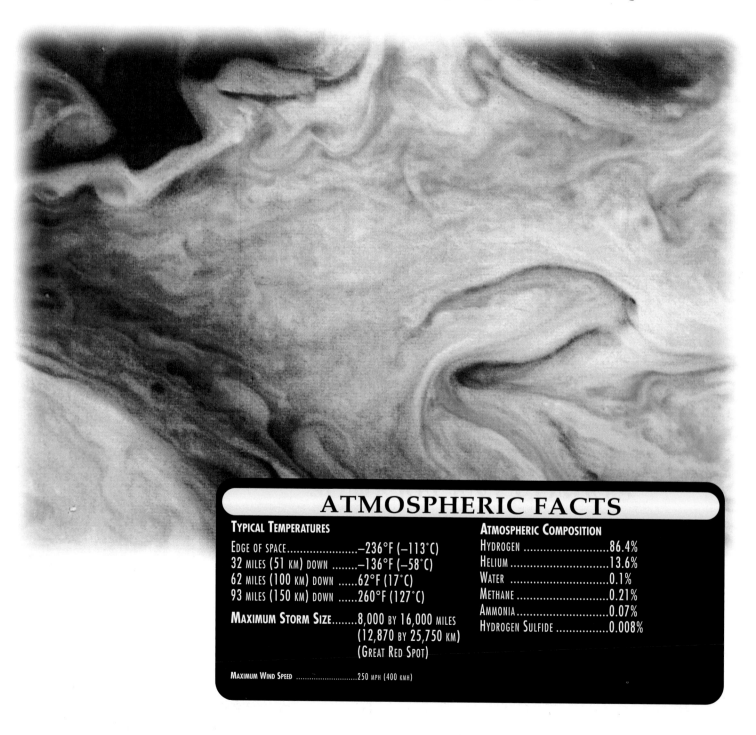

ATMOSPHERIC FACTS

TYPICAL TEMPERATURES

EDGE OF SPACE	−236°F (−113°C)
32 MILES (51 KM) DOWN	−136°F (−58°C)
62 MILES (100 KM) DOWN	62°F (17°C)
93 MILES (150 KM) DOWN	260°F (127°C)

MAXIMUM STORM SIZE........8,000 BY 16,000 MILES (12,870 BY 25,750 KM) (GREAT RED SPOT)

MAXIMUM WIND SPEED ....250 MPH (400 KMH)

ATMOSPHERIC COMPOSITION

HYDROGEN	86.4%
HELIUM	13.6%
WATER	0.1%
METHANE	0.21%
AMMONIA	0.07%
HYDROGEN SULFIDE	0.008%

LIQUID SKY

Like all the gas giants, Jupiter is a spinning sphere of liquid. There is no "surface" at the planet's center—the atmosphere simply gets thicker the deeper it goes, until the pressure is so great that it causes gases to turn into liquid, becoming unlike anything we would call an atmosphere.

Jupiter's atmosphere is made up mainly of hydrogen with lesser amounts of helium, making it very similar to the Sun. If it were a lot bigger, nuclear reactions could start in Jupiter's center and cause it to burn like a star. It is the smaller amounts of heavier elements that cause cloud layers to form high in the atmosphere.

The winds are much stronger on Jupiter than on Earth. Without geographical features to get in the way, the winds whip around the huge globe in distinct weather bands. These bands stay in the same latitudes and have done so for at least 90 years—as long as astronomers have been using modern telescopes.

STORMY WEATHER

Jupiter is famous for the storms that move relentlessly within the different bands. But the most famous storm of all, the Great Red Spot, is big enough to hold up to three whole Earths and has been twirling around Jupiter for at least 150 years—and shows no signs of disappearing. Just as on Earth, Jupiter's violent weather is powered by heat. As gas warms, it expands and rises, creating eddies and swirls. Warm plumes rising from Jupiter's boiling interior cause storms. In turn, these storms create turbulence that powers the banded jet streams in their endless rotation.

The space age may have revealed many new aspects of Jupiter's atmosphere, but there is still much more to learn.

WHAT IF?

...WE COULD WATCH THE *GALILEO* PROBE DESCEND?

December 7, 1995: *Galileo* has just woken from cruising mode. It soon begins a kamikaze dive into Jupiter's atmosphere, falling at a top speed of 106,000 mph (170,590 kmh), causing the plasma in its path to heat to a temperature of 28,000°F (15,537°C).

Parachutes deploy after 170 seconds and the probe begins a more leisurely descent. Swirling layers of cloud and ammonia ice mean the temperature dips to a frigid –238°F (–114°C), but it will increase as the probe continues its descent. As it drops deeper, the winds become fiercer, and the probe is buffeted mercilessly.

Sinking deeper still, the probe is now getting very hot. Eventually, having traveled 400 miles (645 km) through the atmosphere, it ceases to transmit. A few miles farther down, the probe starts to melt. But far above, the waiting orbiter has received its signals—the first ever sent from inside a gas giant and prepares to beam them back to the Earth.

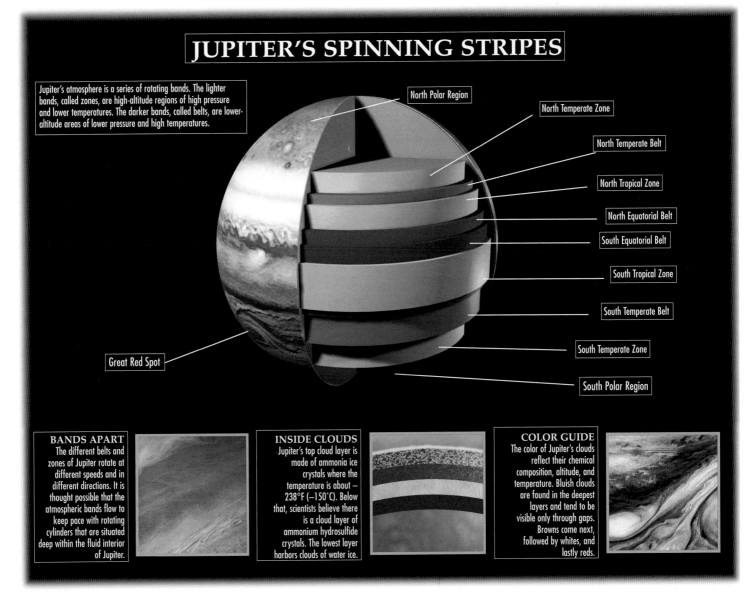

JUPITER'S SPINNING STRIPES

Jupiter's atmosphere is a series of rotating bands. The lighter bands, called zones, are high-altitude regions of high pressure and lower temperatures. The darker bands, called belts, are lower-altitude areas of lower pressure and high temperatures.

North Polar Region
North Temperate Zone
North Temperate Belt
North Tropical Zone
North Equatorial Belt
South Equatorial Belt
South Tropical Zone
South Temperate Belt
South Temperate Zone
South Polar Region
Great Red Spot

BANDS APART
The different belts and zones of Jupiter rotate at different speeds and in different directions. It is thought possible that the atmospheric bands flow to keep pace with rotating cylinders that are situated deep within the fluid interior of Jupiter.

INSIDE CLOUDS
Jupiter's top cloud layer is made of ammonia ice crystals where the temperature is about –238°F (–150°C). Below that, scientists believe there is a cloud layer of ammonium hydrosulfide crystals. The lowest layer harbors clouds of water ice.

COLOR GUIDE
The color of Jupiter's clouds reflect their chemical composition, altitude, and temperature. Bluish clouds are found in the deepest layers and tend to be visible only through gaps. Browns come next, followed by whites, and lastly reds.

JUPITER'S MOON SYSTEM

A grand total of sixty-seven moons are known to orbit the giant planet Jupiter. The four largest moons were discovered by Galileo in the seventeenth century, but nearly three hundred years passed before the fifth was found. Amalthea—and Jupiter's other small moons—proved to be nothing like the larger Galilean satellites. The lumpy, irregularly shaped objects are more like asteroids than moons and they may well be captured asteriods. Their tiny size and great distance from Earth make them hard to study. Only visits by the *Voyager 1* and *Galileo* spacecraft

MINOR MOON ROUNDUP

Name	Diameter	Mean Distance from Center of Jupiter	Orbital Inclination	Discovery Date
Metis	37 x 21 miles (60 x 34 km)	79,510 miles (127,960 km)	0°*	1979
Adrastea	16 x 12 x 9 miles (26 x 19 x 14 km)	80,140 miles (128,973 km)	0°*	1979
Amalthea	155 x 80 miles (249 x 129 km)	112,650 miles (181,293 km)	0.4°	1892
Thebe	72 x 52 miles (116 x 84 km)	137,880 miles (221,896 km)	0.8°*	1979
Leda	68 miles (109 km)	6,893,000 miles (11,093.208 km)	27°	1974
Himalia	106 miles (171 km)*	7,133,000 miles (11,479,451 km)	28°	1904
Lysithea	15 miles (24 km) *	7,282,000 miles (11,719,243 km)	29°	1938
Elara	50 miles (80 km)*	7,293,000 miles (11,736,946 km)	28°	1905
Ananke	12 miles (19 km)*	13,200,000 miles (21,243,341 km)	147°	1951
Carme	19 miles (31 km)*	14,000,000 miles (22,530,816 km)	163°	1938
Pasiphae	22 miles (35 km)*	14,600,000 miles (23,496,422 km)	148°	1908
Sinope	17 miles (27 km)*	14,700,000 miles (23,657,357 km)	153°	1914

*UNCERTAIN

JUPITER'S DISORDERLY MOONS

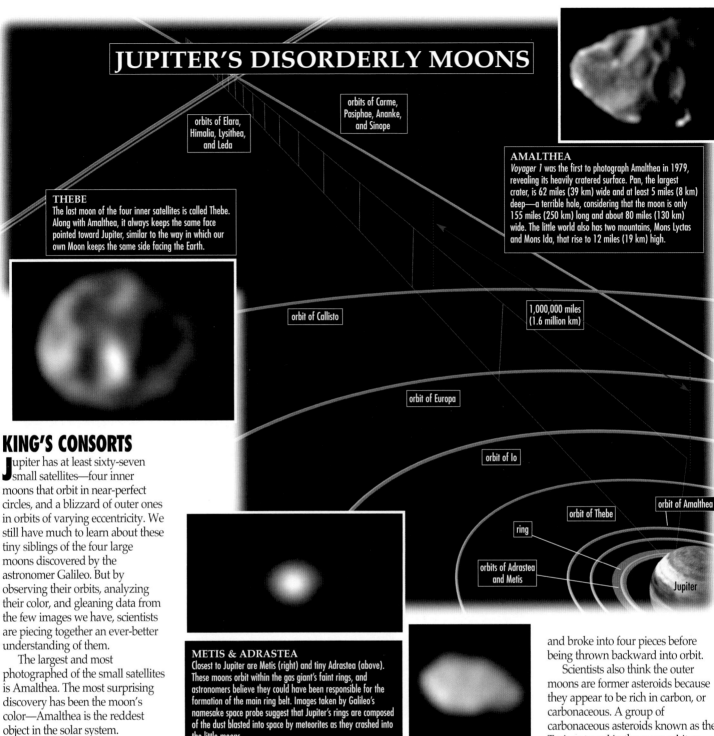

orbits of Elara, Himalia, Lysithea, and Leda

orbits of Carme, Pasiphae, Ananke, and Sinope

THEBE
The last moon of the four inner satellites is called Thebe. Along with Amalthea, it always keeps the same face pointed toward Jupiter, similar to the way in which our own Moon keeps the same side facing the Earth.

AMALTHEA
Voyager 1 was the first to photograph Amalthea in 1979, revealing its heavily cratered surface. Pan, the largest crater, is 62 miles (39 km) wide and at least 5 miles (8 km) deep—a terrible hole, considering that the moon is only 155 miles (250 km) long and about 80 miles (130 km) wide. The little world also has two mountains, Mons Lyctas and Mons Ida, that rise to 12 miles (19 km) high.

orbit of Callisto

1,000,000 miles (1.6 million km)

orbit of Europa

orbit of Io

orbit of Amalthea

orbit of Thebe

ring

orbits of Adrastea and Metis

Jupiter

METIS & ADRASTEA
Closest to Jupiter are Metis (right) and tiny Adrastea (above). These moons orbit within the gas giant's faint rings, and astronomers believe they could have been responsible for the formation of the main ring belt. Images taken by Galileo's namesake space probe suggest that Jupiter's rings are composed of the dust blasted into space by meteorites as they crashed into the little moons.

KING'S CONSORTS

Jupiter has at least sixty-seven small satellites—four inner moons that orbit in near-perfect circles, and a blizzard of outer ones in orbits of varying eccentricity. We still have much to learn about these tiny siblings of the four large moons discovered by the astronomer Galileo. But by observing their orbits, analyzing their color, and gleaning data from the few images we have, scientists are piecing together an ever-better understanding of them.

The largest and most photographed of the small satellites is Amalthea. The most surprising discovery has been the moon's color—Amalthea is the reddest object in the solar system. Astronomers believe the color comes from a layer of sulfur ejected from Io's violent volcanoes. The extremely active Io hurls vast quantities of material into space, and its volcanic substances fall in a stream toward Jupiter. Caught in its path, Amalthea is splattered red. But even odder than its red coating are the mysterious green patches that appear on the major slopes. At present, these are unexplained.

Thebe, Metis, and Adrastea, the remaining inner moons, were caught on camera by *Voyager 1* during its 1979 flyby of Jupiter, but were not photographed properly

until the *Galileo* probe arrived in the 1990s.

Around the same time, improvements to Earth-based telescopes led to a boom in the numbers of irregular outer satellites known to orbit all of the outer planets. We know even less about Jupiter's outer moons, orbiting beyond Callisto, than we do about the inner moons. One group, clustered at about 7 million miles (11.2 million km) from Jupiter, circle in the normal direction—that is, the same way the planet spins. An outer group of moons lying at

about 14 million miles (22 million km) have wild, elliptical orbits and retrograde rotation—in other words, they orbit backward. This backward motion adds weight to the theory that Jupiter's small outer moons are captured asteroids. An asteroid could have come from any direction, and would have had a 50 percent chance of ending up in a backward orbit. Moons that formed along with their parent planet, on the other hand, orbit in the same direction as the planet rotates. It could be that a large asteroid hurtled toward Jupiter

and broke into four pieces before being thrown backward into orbit.

Scientists also think the outer moons are former asteroids because they appear to be rich in carbon, or carbonaceous. A group of carbonaceous asteroids known as the Trojans travel in the same orbit as Jupiter, but always ahead of, or behind, the planet by 60° of the orbit. So the moons could well be escaped Trojans. However, we may have to wait many years before another robot visitor to the Jupiter system can help us shed more light on the problem of the moons' origins. NASA's *New Horizons* probe flew past Jupiter and its moons in February 2007 on its way to explore the dwarf planet Pluto, but it might yet be some time in the future before another robotic visitor arrives on the scene specifically to take pictures of the other outer worlds.

SATURN

Saturn is an enormous globe of whirling gas—it is made almost entirely of hydrogen and helium—that sits at the center of a complex system of rings and at least sixty-two moons. The planet and its companions are almost a solar system in miniature. Saturn's rings, which are composed of billions of separate particles and are usually visible in even a small telescope, long ago earned the planet the title "jewel of the solar system." But it was not until the *Voyager* probes reached the planet in the 1970s that astronomers (and everyone else who marveled at the glorious images) were able to take a closer look at the ringed planet and begin to unlock its mysteries.

SATURN PROFILE

SATURN		EARTH
74,898 miles (120,537 km)	DIAMETER	7,973 miles (12,831 km)
26° 42'	AXIS TILT	23° 27'
10,760 days (29.46 Earth years)	LENGTH OF YEAR	365 days
10 hours 39.4 minutes	LENGTH OF DAY	24 hours
888 million miles (14.3 million km)	DISTANCE FROM SUN	93.5 million miles (150 million km)
−292°F (−144°C)	SURFACE TEMPERATURE	59°F (15°C)
0.93 G	SURFACE GRAVITY	1 G
HYDROGEN (97%), HELIUM (3%), METHANE (0.05%)	ATMOSPHERE	NITROGEN (80%), OXYGEN (19%)
1,400 millibars	ATMOSPHERIC PRESSURE	1,000 millibars
HYDROGEN (97%), HELIUM (3%), METHANE (0.05%)	COMPOSITION	SILICON (60%), ALUMINUM (15%)

LORD OF THE RINGS

Ever since Galileo pointed his crude telescope at the giant planet back in 1610, Saturn's extraordinary rings have been recognized as a marvel of the solar system. But the planet itself, although less spectacular, is almost as extraordinary. Second only to Jupiter in scale, it is 750 times the size of the Earth.

From space, we can observe only the cloud tops of the giant planet, and even these are often obscured by a yellow haze. The entire atmosphere is divided into distinct bands, similar to Jupiter but not so clearly marked. These cloud bands whirl round the planet in jet streams blowing at up to 1,100 miles (1,770 km) an hour—10 times the speed of an earthly hurricane. Saturn's clouds are a bitterly cold –218°F (–103°C). Those we can see are no more than a frosting of ammonia ice on a huge mass of hydrogen and helium below.

There is nowhere on Saturn that could be described as a planetary surface. If we could send an indestructible space probe down through the clouds, it would record a steady increase in temperature and pressure. Thousands of miles down, the craft's barometer would register

atmospheric pressure levels a million times higher than those on Earth. The temperature would rise to match, and would soon reach thousands of degrees.

In such extreme conditions, the hydrogen that makes up much of Saturn's atmosphere behaves very strangely. No longer a gas, it turns into something resembling a liquid metal, capable of conducting electricity. But there is no distinct threshold where atmospheric gas ends and an ocean of liquid hydrogen begins. It is likely that beneath the liquid hydrogen is probably a small core of rock, itself in a liquid state.

RINGS AND MOONS

Everything beneath Saturn's cloud tops is hidden from sight. Most of what we know about its interior has been deduced from what we can see of the cloud tops and what we have learned about how the planet behaves.

There is nothing hidden about the rings. Yet these present puzzles of their own. They are composed of billions of little fragments, mainly of ice, ranging from sand-grain size to lumps as big as a house. All of them orbit

independently, engaged in an almost fantastically complex dance that is brought to some kind of order by the gravitational pull of Saturn's moons.

These, too, hold unsolved mysteries. Why is Iapetus half-blackened, and how did little Mimas acquire a crater a third the size of the entire moon? The *Cassini* spacecraft, which arrived at Saturn in 2004, is helping to solve some of these mysteries through a series of flybys of the Saturnian moons, currently expected to last until 2017.

FLOATER

SATURN IS THE ONLY PLANET IN THE SOLAR SYSTEM LESS DENSE THAN WATER. IF YOU COULD FIND A TUB BIG ENOUGH TO DUNK IT IN, THE GIANT WOULD FLOAT ON THE TOP LIKE AN APPLE IN A WATER BARREL. IN FACT, AT ONLY 69 PERCENT THAT OF FRESH WATER, SATURN'S AVERAGE DENSITY IS MUCH THE SAME AS MANY APPLES. BY COMPARISON, THE EARTH IS ALMOST EIGHT TIMES AS DENSE AS ITS MUCH BIGGER NEIGHBOR.

SQUASHED

SATURN IS THE MOST FLATTENED PLANET IN THE SOLAR SYSTEM. ITS DIAMETER AT THE EQUATOR IS 74,898 MILES (120,540 KM), BUT ONLY 67,560 MILES (108,730 KM) MEASURED POLE TO POLE. THE EQUATORIAL BULGE IS CAUSED BY THE CENTRIFUGAL FORCE OF THE PLANET'S RAPID ROTATION: SATURN MAKES A COMPLETE REVOLUTION IN JUST 10.5 HOURS. EVEN OUR SLOWER-TURNING EARTH HAS A SLIGHT BULGE AT THE EQUATOR, AND EARTH IS A RIGID, ROCKY WORLD, NOT A GIANT BALL OF GAS.

SATURN'S MOONS

PORTRAIT OF A GIANT

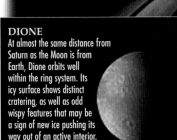

IAPETUS
In a contrast as startling as soot on snow, half of the 900-mile-diameter (1,450-km-diameter) moon is dark and half bright. The dark hemisphere always leads in Iapetus's orbit around Saturn. The "soot" is probably a thin layer of space debris.

TETHYS
A ball of near-pure ice, Tethys has a 1,200-mile (1,930 km) chasm running over its cratered surface. It may be the result of water freezing inside the moon and cracking its crust.

DIONE
At almost the same distance from Saturn as the Moon is from Earth, Dione orbits well within the ring system. Its icy surface shows distinct cratering, as well as odd wispy features that may be a sign of new ice pushing its way out of an active interior.

Tethys's shadow

ENCELADUS
The brightest moon in the solar system, Enceladus reflects almost 100 percent of the sunlight that reaches it. Since it absorbs so little, its surface is the coldest part of Saturn's system, with a temperature of –392°F (–200°C). Tides driven by Saturn's gravity may stir the moon's interior.

URANUS

The giant blue-green globe of Uranus is big enough to swallow the Earth sixty-four times over. It has a strong magnetic field, a family of at least twenty-seven moons, and, after Saturn, the most impressive system of rings in the solar system. Beneath its smooth-looking, almost featureless exterior, Uranus is essentially a fluid world. An atmosphere rich in hydrogen thickens imperceptibly, with no discernible break between gas and liquid, into a worldwide ocean where water and methane predominate.

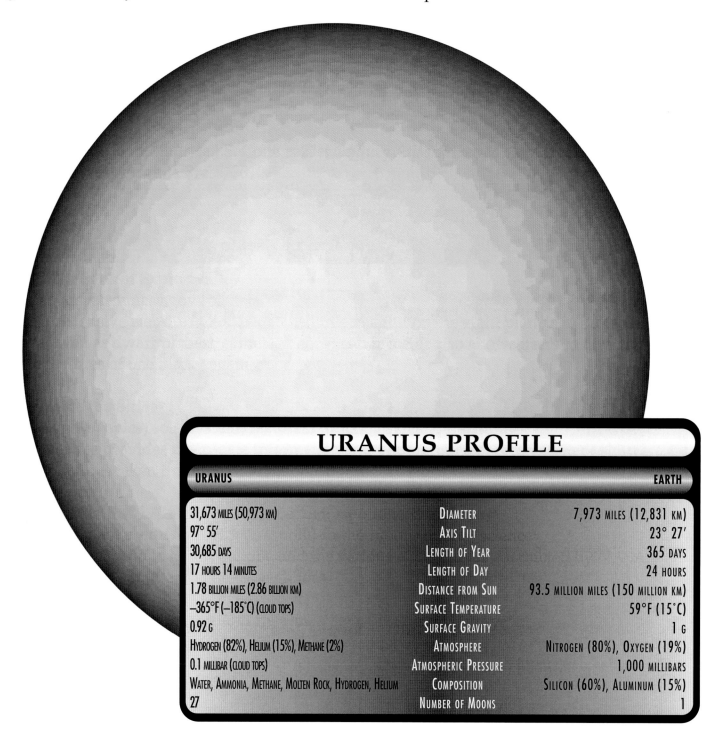

URANUS PROFILE

URANUS		EARTH
31,673 MILES (50,973 KM)	DIAMETER	7,973 MILES (12,831 KM)
97° 55'	AXIS TILT	23° 27'
30,685 DAYS	LENGTH OF YEAR	365 DAYS
17 HOURS 14 MINUTES	LENGTH OF DAY	24 HOURS
1.78 BILLION MILES (2.86 BILLION KM)	DISTANCE FROM SUN	93.5 MILLION MILES (150 MILLION KM)
−365°F (−185°C) (CLOUD TOPS)	SURFACE TEMPERATURE	59°F (15°C)
0.92 G	SURFACE GRAVITY	1 G
HYDROGEN (82%), HELIUM (15%), METHANE (2%)	ATMOSPHERE	NITROGEN (80%), OXYGEN (19%)
0.1 MILLIBAR (CLOUD TOPS)	ATMOSPHERIC PRESSURE	1,000 MILLIBARS
WATER, AMMONIA, METHANE, MOLTEN ROCK, HYDROGEN, HELIUM	COMPOSITION	SILICON (60%), ALUMINUM (15%)
27	NUMBER OF MOONS	1

GREEN GIANT

Uranus is a giant planet—four times the diameter of the Earth—but it is so far away that it is all but invisible to the naked eye. So although the planets in the solar system out to Saturn have been known since antiquity, Uranus was not discovered until 1781. Its discovery doubled the dimensions of the known solar system, but astronomers knew little of this huge world until the *Voyager 2* probe passed within 51,000 miles (82,077 km) of it on January 24, 1986—almost two centuries after its discovery.

The images sent back by *Voyager 2* were somewhat surprising. No surface details of Uranus can be seen from Earth, but even close up, *Voyager* could see only a featureless blue-green globe. The planet has none of the strikingly colored atmospheric bands typical of Saturn and Jupiter, even though, like these two worlds, its atmosphere is composed almost entirely of hydrogen and helium.

Voyager 2 did show that the atmosphere on Uranus has a band-like structure, but it can only be seen clearly in high-contrast false-color images. Uranus is so cold that its clouds form very low down, their colors hidden from view by the blue-green atmosphere above them.

LIQUID GAS

The interior of Uranus is also unlike those of Saturn and Jupiter, which consist mainly of hydrogen. Its density is higher, a sign that heavier gases and liquid are present. Although Uranus is

often called a gas giant, its actual composition is almost certainly mainly liquid—hydrogen makes up only 15 percent of the planet's mass, compared with more than 80 percent of Jupiter's, and almost all of it is in the atmosphere. Uranus probably has a rocky core surrounded by an ocean of water, liquid methane, and liquid hydrogen. The ocean—hot, under the prevailing pressure— gradually blends into the atmosphere. Like all the other gas giants, Uranus has no distinct surface to separate the point at which "air" becomes "ground."

The rings of Uranus were first seen in 1977 when the planet passed in front of a background star. The star appeared to flicker as it went behind the planet, a sign that something was blocking its

light. Earthbound telescopes detected a total of nine rings; the *Voyager 2* mission found two more. They are all very narrow and dark, typically as black as coal; and like those of Saturn, the material they are made of ranges in size from dust specks to rocky

lumps up to 30 feet (9 m) across. The innermost ring, designated 1986U2R by astronomers, is about 24,000 miles (38,620 km) from the center of Uranus. The outermost and brightest ring—Epsilon—is around 6,000 miles (9,650 km) farther out.

water, liquid methane, and liquid hydrogen

rocky core

atmosphere of hydrogen, helium, and methane

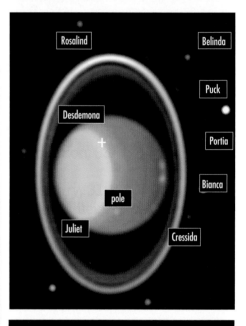

Rosalind | Belinda

Puck

Desdemona

Portia

Bianca

pole

Juliet

Cressida

MOONS
Until the *Voyager 2* encounter with Uranus, only five moons of Uranus were known; two were found in 1787 (Titania and Oberon), two in 1850 (Ariel and Umbriel), and the last as recently as 1948 (Miranda). Most are named after characters from the works of William Shakespeare. *Voyager 2* found another 10 (of which eight are visible in this false-color picture), and in 1997, Earth-based telescopes found 12 more, bringing the total up to 27.

RINGS
Uranus has 11 rings, nine of which were detected from Earth. The other two were discovered in 1986 by *Voyager 2*. This probe also found 10 new moons, two of which act as "shepherd moons" and keep the outer ring, Epsilon, in position.

URANUS: ITS RINGS AND MOONS

NEPTUNE

Remote Neptune, the eighth and farthest planet in the solar system, was unknown until a century and a half ago. Its year is so long that it has still not completed a full orbit of the Sun since it was discovered. Earthbound observers knew almost nothing about Neptune until the NASA *Voyager 2* probe passed by the planet in 1989 and returned spectacular views of this mysterious blue world. But although *Voyager 2* established that the planet shares many family characteristics with Jupiter, Saturn, and Uranus, Neptune has yet to give up its greatest secret: the source of the unimaginable heat that rises from the planet's center to drive the violent winds

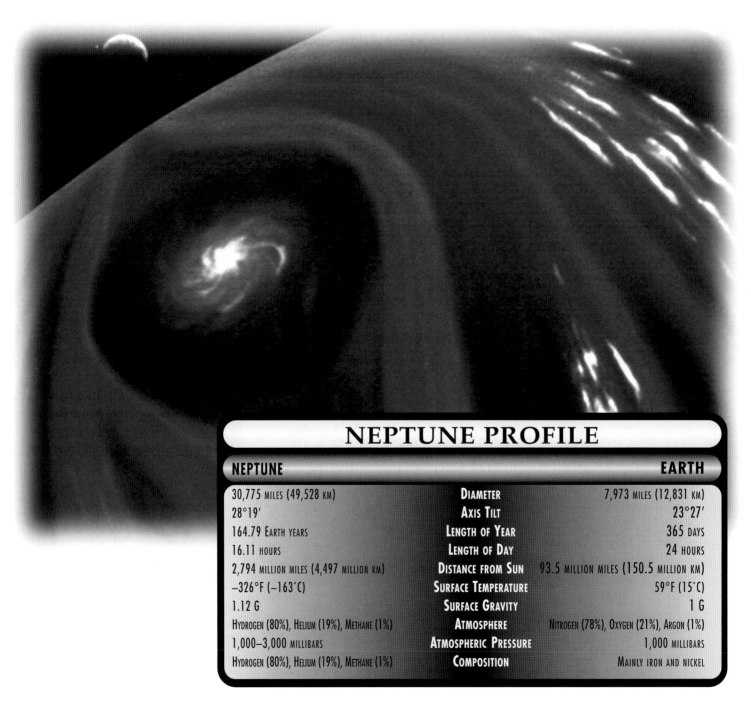

NEPTUNE PROFILE

NEPTUNE		EARTH
30,775 miles (49,528 km)	DIAMETER	7,973 miles (12,831 km)
28°19'	AXIS TILT	23°27'
164.79 Earth years	LENGTH OF YEAR	365 days
16.11 hours	LENGTH OF DAY	24 hours
2,794 million miles (4,497 million km)	DISTANCE FROM SUN	93.5 million miles (150.5 million km)
−326°F (−163°C)	SURFACE TEMPERATURE	59°F (15°C)
1.12 G	SURFACE GRAVITY	1 G
Hydrogen (80%), Helium (19%), Methane (1%)	ATMOSPHERE	Nitrogen (78%), Oxygen (21%), Argon (1%)
1,000–3,000 millibars	ATMOSPHERIC PRESSURE	1,000 millibars
Hydrogen (80%), Helium (19%), Methane (1%)	COMPOSITION	Mainly iron and nickel

THE BIG BLUE

The blue-green globe of Neptune keeps a silent watch over the outer reaches of the solar system as it follows its leisurely 168-year orbit around the Sun. Little Pluto, its rocky partner Charon, and a host of unknown comets lie beyond, but Neptune is the last of the orderly pattern that comprises the four inner rocky planets—Mercury, Venus, Earth, and Mars—and the four outer gas giants—Jupiter, Saturn, Uranus, and Neptune itself.

Neptune is so far away from the Sun—about 2.8 billion miles (4.5 billion km) on average—that it is too dim for the naked eye to see. Even the most powerful Earth-based telescopes reveal hardly any details of the surface. To find out more, NASA dispatched the *Voyager 2* mission to take a closer look. The spacecraft hurtled past the planet in 1989, closing to within about 3,000 miles (5,000 km) of the cloud tops of Neptune's thick, hazardous atmosphere.

The Neptunian atmosphere accounts for most of the planet's bulk. It is constantly tormented by winds that blow at up to 1,500 mph (2,400 kmh) and by giant, fast-moving storms like the Great Dark Spot that was identified by the *Voyager 2* probe.

Atmospheric activity on this scale requires colossal amounts of energy, but the source of this energy is one of the Blue Planet's greatest mysteries. On Earth, our weather is driven by heat from the Sun. Neptune's remote orbit is thirty times farther out from the Sun, which causes solar radiation to dwindle to less than one nine-hundredth of Earth levels. Neptune is also farther from the Sun than Uranus, yet astronomers know that it is warmer. So where does the energy come from?

CRUSHED HEAT

Neptune's heat can only be generated from within the planet itself. The most popular theory is that materials of different densities within the interior have yet to fully separate out—that the planet's gravity is still dragging heavier matter toward the core, creating friction that in turn generates heat.

Scientists have speculated that such enormous heat and pressure would cause the methane at Neptune's core to separate into its component elements—hydrogen and carbon—and that the pressure might compress the carbon into a form familiar to us all: diamonds.

ATMOSPHERE
This makes up most of the planet's bulk and is roughly 80 percent hydrogen and 19 percent helium. It is a violently energetic environment, almost certainly due to the heat radiating from the core.

DARK SPOT
Voyager 2 revealed a giant storm system (right), dubbed the Great Dark Spot, Neptune's southern hemisphere. The Spot was estimated to be about the same size as the Earth and rotated counterclockwise. Above the Spot drifted feathery white clouds that resembled the cirrus clouds in the Earth's atmosphere.

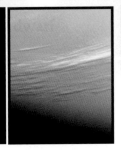
THE SCOOTER
Voyager 2 sent back pictures of a small, bright, eastward-moving cloud that scientists dubbed "the Scooter" (above). True to its name, the cloud scooted around Neptune every 16 hours, blown by the planet's strong winds. Small streaks within the Scooter constantly caused its appearance to change.

CLOUDS

Neptune's wispy clouds consist of frozen methane crystals high in the atmosphere. The planet's blue-green color is due to the presence of methane in the thicker cloud layers below. These layers also contain crystals of ammonia and hydrogen sulfide, and display banding similar to the clouds on Jupiter and Saturn.

GIANT OCEAN
Scientists speculate that beneath the Neptunian atmosphere lies a planet-wide ocean of water, liquid ammonia, and methane. Even at "sea level," its temperature is a staggeringly hot 4,000°F (2,204°C). It is the enormous pressure of Neptune's atmosphere that keeps the ocean liquid.

MOLTEN CORE

In common with most of the gas giants, Neptune may have a small, molten core consisting of mainly iron and silicon compounds. The temperature near the core is thought to be over 12,000°F (6,649°C).

NEPTUNE INSIDE AND OUT

PLUTO AND CHARON

Pluto, the outermost known planet in the solar system—reclassified as a dwarf planet in 2006—orbits the Sun once every 248 years at a distance of up to 4.6 billion miles (7.4 billion km). Its largest moon, Charon, is so similar in size that together they make up the solar system's only double planet, but they are so far from Earth that very little surface detail has been discovered. Despite the lack of data, astronomers know that Pluto is an icy, rocky world and even—at times—has an atmosphere. But there is still much to learn.

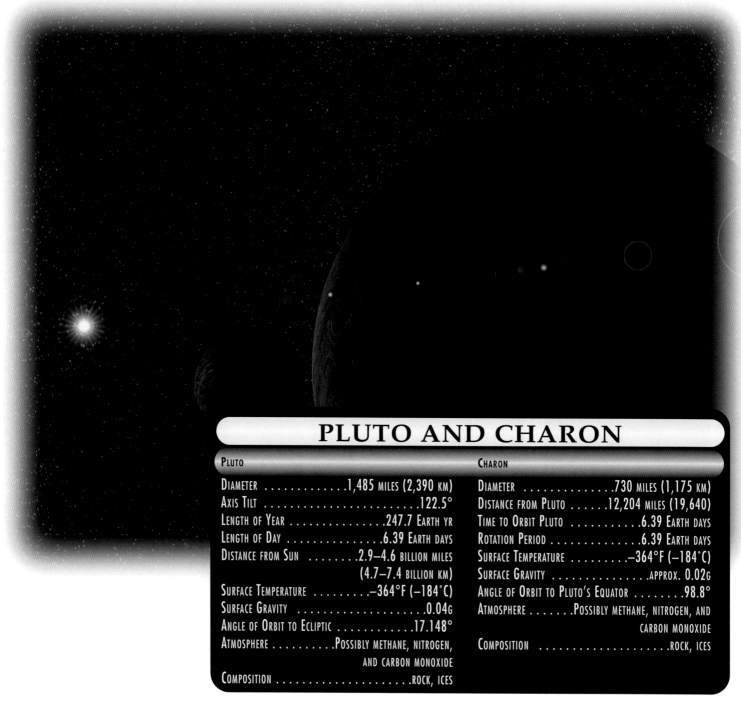

PLUTO AND CHARON

PLUTO		CHARON	
DIAMETER	.1,485 MILES (2,390 KM)	DIAMETER	.730 MILES (1,175 KM)
AXIS TILT	.122.5°	DISTANCE FROM PLUTO	.12,204 MILES (19,640)
LENGTH OF YEAR	.247.7 EARTH YR	TIME TO ORBIT PLUTO	.6.39 EARTH DAYS
LENGTH OF DAY	.6.39 EARTH DAYS	ROTATION PERIOD	.6.39 EARTH DAYS
DISTANCE FROM SUN	.2.9–4.6 BILLION MILES (4.7–7.4 BILLION KM)	SURFACE TEMPERATURE	.–364°F (–184°C)
		SURFACE GRAVITY	.APPROX. 0.02G
SURFACE TEMPERATURE	.–364°F (–184°C)	ANGLE OF ORBIT TO PLUTO'S EQUATOR	.98.8°
SURFACE GRAVITY	.0.04G	ATMOSPHERE	.POSSIBLY METHANE, NITROGEN, AND CARBON MONOXIDE
ANGLE OF ORBIT TO ECLIPTIC	.17.148°		
ATMOSPHERE	.POSSIBLY METHANE, NITROGEN, AND CARBON MONOXIDE	COMPOSITION	.ROCK, ICES
COMPOSITION	.ROCK, ICES		

DISTANT ICEBALLS

Astronomers know very little about Pluto. It is simply too far away, not to mention too small, for even space-based telescopes to reveal much, and it is the only planet yet to be visited by a space probe. But even with the scant information available, it is clear that the dwarf Pluto is the oddball of the solar system.

Pluto is easily the smallest of the known planets. It is just one-fifth the diameter of Earth and smaller than the solar system's seven largest planetary satellites, including the Earth's own Moon. In fact, Pluto is so tiny that many astronomers originally thought that it was really an escaped moon that had once orbited Neptune. Further evidence for the escaped-moon theory came from Pluto's orbit around the Sun, which is quite unlike that of any other planet and suggests that Pluto entered its present orbit long after the other planets settled into theirs.

Pluto's orbit is the most elongated ellipse of any of the planets. At its most distant from the Sun—4.6 billion miles (7.4 billion km)—Pluto is almost 2 billion miles (3.2 billion km) farther out than when it is at its closest, at which point it passes nearer to the Sun than its neighbor Neptune does. Stranger still, Pluto's orbit is tilted at an angle of some 17° to the orbits of all the other planets.

But in 1978, the discovery that Pluto had a satellite cast doubt on the "escaped moon" theory. As an alternative, some astronomers have suggested that Pluto, and its largest companion Charon, originated in the Kuiper Belt—the distant ring of rocky and icy debris that extends beyond the orbit of Neptune.

NEVER FAR APART

Pluto and Charon are sometimes labeled the "dwarf double planet" because their sizes are closer together than most planet-moon combinations, and the distance between them is far less. Charon is more than half the diameter of Pluto—making it the largest moon in relation to its parent planet—and it orbits its parent at a distance of only about eight Pluto diameters. By comparison, in the Earth-Moon system, the Moon is just over a quarter of the Earth's diameter and separated by thirty-one Earth diameters.

Pluto's surface is probably covered in frozen nitrogen, methane, and carbon monoxide, which vaporize to form a very thin atmosphere when the planet moves closest to the Sun. Charon, by contrast, may have water ice on its surface. But we did not know for sure until the double planet was visited by a space probe—the *New Horizons* probe flew past Pluto in 2015.

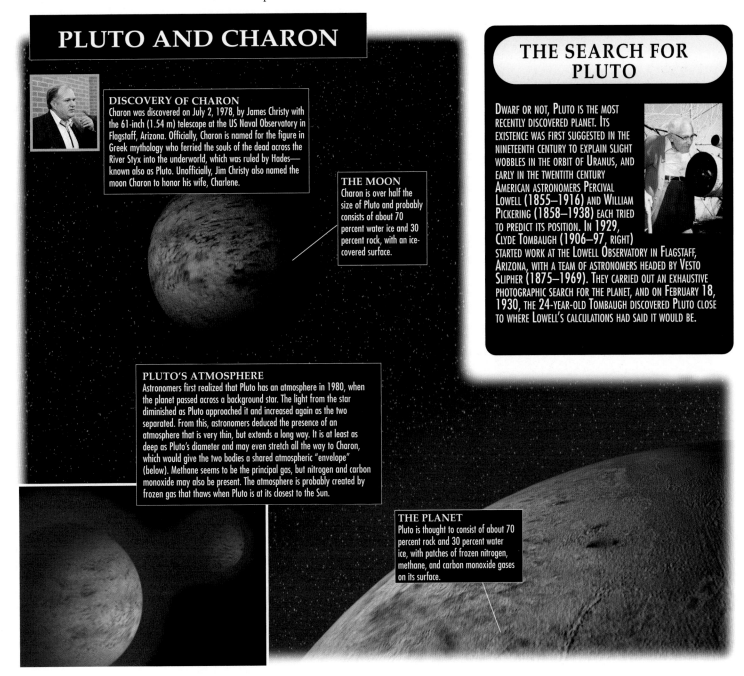

PLUTO AND CHARON

DISCOVERY OF CHARON
Charon was discovered on July 2, 1978, by James Christy with the 61-inch (1.54 m) telescope at the US Naval Observatory in Flagstaff, Arizona. Officially, Charon is named for the figure in Greek mythology who ferried the souls of the dead across the River Styx into the underworld, which was ruled by Hades—known also as Pluto. Unofficially, Jim Christy also named the moon Charon to honor his wife, Charlene.

THE MOON
Charon is over half the size of Pluto and probably consists of about 70 percent water ice and 30 percent rock, with an ice-covered surface.

PLUTO'S ATMOSPHERE
Astronomers first realized that Pluto has an atmosphere in 1980, when the planet passed across a background star. The light from the star diminished as Pluto approached it and increased again as the two separated. From this, astronomers deduced the presence of an atmosphere that is very thin, but extends a long way. It is at least as deep as Pluto's diameter and may even stretch all the way to Charon, which would give the two bodies a shared atmospheric "envelope" (below). Methane seems to be the principal gas, but nitrogen and carbon monoxide may also be present. The atmosphere is probably created by frozen gas that thaws when Pluto is at its closest to the Sun.

THE PLANET
Pluto is thought to consist of about 70 percent rock and 30 percent water ice, with patches of frozen nitrogen, methane, and carbon monoxide gases on its surface.

THE SEARCH FOR PLUTO
Dwarf or not, Pluto is the most recently discovered planet. Its existence was first suggested in the nineteenth century to explain slight wobbles in the orbit of Uranus, and early in the twentieth century American astronomers Percival Lowell (1855–1916) and William Pickering (1858–1938) each tried to predict its position. In 1929, Clyde Tombaugh (1906–97, right) started work at the Lowell Observatory in Flagstaff, Arizona, with a team of astronomers headed by Vesto Slipher (1875–1969). They carried out an exhaustive photographic search for the planet, and on February 18, 1930, the 24-year-old Tombaugh discovered Pluto close to where Lowell's calculations had said it would be.

BEYOND PLUTO

Fifty years ago, at the beginning of the space age, Pluto was routinely described as the most distant object in the solar system. However, recent discoveries and theories suggest that the planets occupy just the inner heart. Four probes have now traveled to about twice the distance of Pluto, into the realm of the comets, with others likely to follow. Eventually, all these probes will travel through the solar system's outer reaches, where lonely comets orbit the Sun—three-quarters of the way to the nearest star.

NEW HORIZONS SCHEDULE

JANUARY 2006	Launched
APRIL 2006	Mars
JUNE 2008	Saturn
MARCH 2011	Uranus
JULY 2015	Pluto/Charon
2015–2020	first Kuiper Belt encounters
2020 onward	possible extended mission

TO THE EDGE

Astronomers are eager to establish the boundaries to the Sun's empire. There are two possible answers. One depends on the extent of the Sun's electromagnetic influence, the other on its gravitational reach. The electromagnetic influence—the solar wind, as it is called—gradually fades as it encounters the dust, gas, and radiation that make up the incredibly tenuous "atmosphere" between the stars, known as the interstellar medium. *Pioneer 10* and *Voyager 1*, both at almost twice Pluto's distance, report that the intensity of cosmic rays from other stars increases by 1.3 percent every 100 million miles (160 million km). At that rate, like the light of a lighthouse dying away in fog, the Sun's radiation should finally fade out at about four times Pluto's distance.

Meanwhile, *Pioneer 10* and *Voyager 1*—along with *Voyager 2*, now 5.5 billion miles (8.9 billion km) away—have entered the domain of the comets. Astronomers believe that the cometary sources form two regions, one that reaches to 25 times the distance of Pluto from the Sun and a second stretching out to 5,000 times that distance.

INTO COMET COUNTRY

The first comet store, the source of short-period comets, is named after Dutch-American astronomer Gerard Kuiper (1905–73), who suggested its existence in 1951. He proposed that the belt stretched from Neptune's orbit to twenty-five times Pluto's distance from the Sun, lying in the same plane as the planets. Until 1992, the Kuiper Belt was mere theory. But then David Jewitt and Jane Luu of the University of California spotted a minute object about 200 miles (320 km) across, orbiting beyond Neptune—the first Kuiper Belt Object (KBO). Since then, some sixty objects have been found. Astronomers theorize that there should be anything from 1 billion to 6.7 billion of them. *Voyager 1*, *Voyager 2*, and *Pioneer 10* are in the Kuiper Belt now. Slight shifts in their path may allow scientists to calculate the combined gravity of the comets and estimate their numbers.

The second comet "sink" is the source of long-period comets, a cloud named for Dutch scientist Jan Oort (1900–92), who suggested its existence in the 1940s. This halo of the solar system, ranging from 6,000 to 200,000 times the distance of Earth to the Sun, may contain as many as six trillion comets. If the *Voyager* and *Pioneer* probes survive long enough to enter the Oort Cloud, it will be as dead objects in 2,000 years. They will probably continue their journey unscathed, leaving the Oort Cloud—and the solar system—some 65,000 years later.

ANOTHER PLANET?

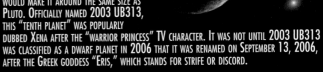

IN JANUARY 2005, ASTRONOMERS MICHAEL BROWN, CHAD TRUJILLO, AND DAVID RABINOWITZ AT THE MOUNT PALOMAR OBSERVATORY IN CALIFORNIA DISCOVERED AN OBJECT BEYOND THE ORBIT OF NEPTUNE WHICH SEEMED TO HAVE A RADIUS OF AROUND 1,420 MILES (2,300 KM). THIS WOULD MAKE IT AROUND THE SAME SIZE AS PLUTO. OFFICIALLY NAMED 2003 UB313, THIS "TENTH PLANET" WAS POPULARLY DUBBED XENA AFTER THE "WARRIOR PRINCESS" TV CHARACTER. IT WAS NOT UNTIL 2003 UB313 WAS CLASSIFIED AS A DWARF PLANET IN 2006 THAT IT WAS RENAMED ON SEPTEMBER 13, 2006, AFTER THE GREEK GODDESS "ERIS," WHICH STANDS FOR STRIFE OR DISCORD.

COMET FARM

THE KUIPER BELT (RIGHT) MAY CONSIST OF UP TO ABOUT 6 BILLION OBJECTS, OF WHICH SOME 70,000 ARE PLANETESIMALS BETWEEN 60 AND 475 MILES (97 AND 764 KM) ACROSS LYING IN A BAND STRETCHING 30 TO 50 AU, 200 MILLION ARE IN THE 6- TO 12-MILE (10- TO 19 KM) SIZE RANGE, AND THE REST ARE UNDER A MILE ACROSS. ANY ONE OF THEM COULD BE NUDGED FROM ITS ORBIT AND BECOME A COMET. DESPITE THEIR NUMBERS, THE DISTANCES BETWEEN THEM ARE IMMENSE—ABOUT ONE LARGE OBJECT EVERY 100 MILLION MILES (160 MILLION KM).

MISSION IMPOSSIBLE?

PLUTO
This is the most detailed image of Pluto (left) that we have. It was taken by the Hubble Space Telescope in 1996. The *New Horizons* probe has supplied us with much more detailed images.

NEPTUNE
This image of Neptune (above) was captured by *Voyager 2* during its encounter with the planet in 1989. Neptune is the most distant of the planets examined by probe so far.

The *New Horizons* mission reached its first objective, Pluto, in 2015. If all goes well, NASA hopes that the intrepid probe will then be able to venture on into the Kuiper Belt and examine some of its icy denizens. It took the probe eight years to reach Pluto from Earth.

ASTEROID BELT

The asteroid belt—a broad band between the orbits of Mars and Jupiter—is home to thousands of small, rocky bodies that orbit the Sun. These asteroids, also called "minor planets," are thought to be the remains of a larger planet that tried to form in the early days of the solar system but was prevented from doing so by the powerful gravitational influence of the giant planet Jupiter. Despite their sinister reputation, the combined mass of the asteroids in the belt is still less than 1 percent of the Earth's mass.

ASTEROID SIZE

ASTEROID NUMBERING

WHEN AN ASTEROID'S ORBITAL DETAILS HAVE BEEN ESTABLISHED, ASTRONOMERS GIVE IT A NUMBER THAT IS WRITTEN BEFORE THE NAME. ASTEROIDS ARE RARELY SPHERICAL. THE SIZES GIVEN BELOW ARE MAXIMUMS.

LARGE ASTEROIDS

ASTEROIDS LARGER THAN 100 MILES (160 KM) ACROSS	.26
ASTEROIDS LARGER THAN 300 FEET (90 M) ACROSS	POSSIBLY 1 MILLION
TOTAL MASS OF ASTEROIDS IN BELT	LESS THAN 15 PERCENT OF THE MOON

VERMIN OF THE SKIES

At the end of the eighteenth century, astronomers began to search for a "missing" planet that they were convinced must exist in the extra-large gap between the orbits of Mars and Jupiter. Among these astronomers was a group that called itself the "Celestial Police."

This group scanned the skies systematically for a dot of light that could be seen to move in relation to the stars. But they were cheated of their quarry. Other astronomers established that the gap between Mars and Jupiter was filled with a number of tiny asteroids rather than the full-sized planet that the Celestial Police hoped to find. The first of these asteroids was discovered on January 1, 1801, by the Italian astronomer Giuseppe Piazzi. He named the new body Ceres, for the Roman goddess of agriculture. A second, Pallas, was found by German astronomer Heinrich Olbers in March 1802.

In the following years, more of these miniature worlds were found. Astronomers now think that there are probably tens of thousands of asteroids—one called them "vermin of the skies"—and over 8,500 have now been cataloged. Hundreds of new asteroids are added to the record every year.

MAVERICK ORBITS

The orbits of most asteroids lie between those of Mars and Jupiter, but there are some asteroids that travel in what are called maverick orbits. Some of these pass closer to the Sun than the Earth, some extend way beyond Jupiter, and others—the Trojan asteroids—travel in the same orbit as Jupiter.

Asteroids have too little gravity to support atmospheres, or even to draw themselves into a spherical shape; most resemble shapes like lumpy potatoes. The majority are also too close to the Sun to have retained any water or methane in frozen form.

Nearly all known asteroids are pitted with craters—the scars of impacts with meteoroids or other asteroids. Most of this probably happened when the solar system was forming and space was more crowded. More recent cratering could be due to a much larger asteroid that broke up.

ASTEROID MOON
Dactyl, the moon of asteroid 243 Ida, was the first satellite of an asteroid to be discovered. It was first imaged by the *Galileo* spacecraft in 1993. Ida is about 36 miles (58 km) long; Dactyl is just 1 mile (1.6 km) long.

CERES
This image of 1 Ceres was taken by the Hubble Space Telescope. Ceres, the first and largest asteroid to be discovered, is almost spherical—unlike any of the other known asteroids. Ceres was also classified as a dwarf planet in 2006, but is still otfen called an asteroid.

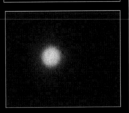

MATHILDE
An image of 253 Mathilde, built from four separate images taken by the *NEAR* (Near-Earth Asteroid Rendezvous) probe in 1997 from a distance of 1,500 miles (2,414 km). The central shadow is a crater thought to be 6 miles (10 km) deep.

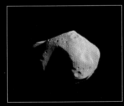

LAGRANGE

THE TROJAN ASTEROIDS TRAVEL IN TWO GROUPS IN THE ORBIT OF JUPITER, ONE 60° AHEAD OF THE PLANET, THE OTHER 60° BEHIND IT. THESE POSITIONS ARE TWO OF WHAT ARE KNOWN AS THE LAGRANGE POINTS OF THE ORBIT. THESE POINTS, AT WHICH SMALL OBJECTS CAN SAFELY REMAIN IN A LARGER OBJECT'S ORBIT, ARE NAMED FOR THE FRENCH ASTRONOMER JOSEPH LAGRANGE (1736–1813), WHO CALCULATED THEIR EXISTENCE MATHEMATICALLY.

NO IMPACT

SCIENCE FICTION WRITERS, BELIEVING THAT ASTEROIDS MUST BE CROWDED TOGETHER IN SPACE, HAVE OFTEN PORTRAYED THE ASTEROID BELT AS A PLACE OF DANGER FOR SPACE TRAVELERS. SOME HAVE EVEN SPECULATED THAT SPACECRAFT ENTERING THE REGION WOULD BE BATTERED BY "ASTEROID STORMS." THE ASTEROID BELT IS CERTAINLY CROWDED, BUT ONLY BY COMPARISON WITH THE REST OF THE SOLAR SYSTEM, WHICH IS A VERY EMPTY PLACE INDEED. THE TWO *PIONEER* AND TWO *VOYAGER* PROBES THAT VISITED THE OUTER PLANETS FLEW THROUGH THE ASTEROID BELT WITHOUT ANY CLOSE ENCOUNTERS.

THE ASTEROID BELT

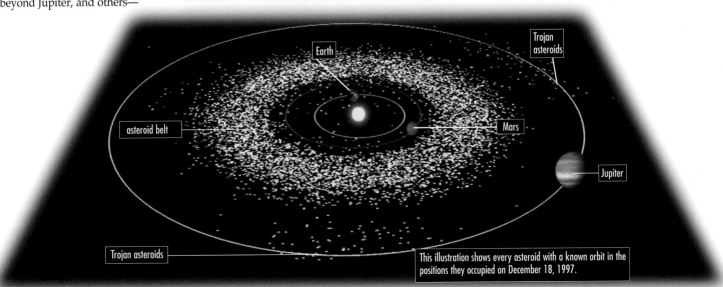

This illustration shows every asteroid with a known orbit in the positions they occupied on December 18, 1997.

COMETS

Comets are really nothing more than small, dirty balls of ice, dust, and rock that swoop around the solar system in elongated, elliptical orbits. In deep space, they are inert; but as they near the inner solar system, the Sun's heat brings them to life. The ice melts, and the dust and gas boil off to form great glowing tails that can stretch tens of millions of miles through space. For thousands of years, comets were thought to herald great events—or, opposingly, ones foretelling doom. Now, some scientists study their composition with interest as they believe comets may harbor the seeds of life itself.

SOME RECENT COMETS

Name	Closest Approach to Sun (million miles / million km)	Date of Closest Approach	Period
Kohoutek	13.1/21	December 28, 1973	6.67
Kobayashi-Berger-Milon	39.6/63.7	September 9, 1975	Not periodic
West	18.3/29.4	February 25, 1976	Not periodic
Encke	31.6/50.9	August 17, 1977	3.3
Halley	54.8/88	February 9, 1986	76.0
Hyakutake	21.4/34.4	May 1, 1996	Not periodic
Hale-Bopp	84.9/136.6	April 1, 1997	2,380
Lovejoy	36.8/59.3	September 7, 2013	6,300

DIRTY SNOWBALLS

Comets were formed along with the rest of the solar system around 4.6 billion years ago. These fragile lumps of ice and frozen gas could never have coalesced anywhere close to the Sun or they would have been quickly evaporated by its heat. Instead, they were probably born much farther out, in the cold vicinity of the orbits of Uranus or Neptune. There, the comets would have been strongly affected by the gravitation of these two planets. Many of them would have been slung far from the planetary realm to form the Oort Cloud—a spherical region of inert comets that surrounds our solar system and reaches perhaps halfway to the nearest star.

Even at that distance, comets remain in orbit around the Sun—although they may take millions of years to complete their long, elliptical journey. A few—classified by astronomers as short-period comets—make a full orbit in less than 200 years. All the rest are grouped together as long-period comets. Often,

they approach from the Oort Cloud at a steep angle to the plane of the planets, and many of them may be on their first visit to the inner solar system. The human race could well be extinct before some of these voyagers return—if they ever do make the journey towards Earth.

Whatever its orbital period, though, every comet spends most of its existence as an insignificant speck of deep-frozen cosmic debris that is invisible even to the most powerful of telescopes. But as the comet begins its approach to the Sun, the growing warmth triggers a miraculous transformation.

COMET STRUCTURE

At the heart of a comet is a nucleus, at most only tens of miles across. Often called a "dirty snowball," it is largely made of ice, sometimes with a rocky core of a few miles across. The ice consists of layers of frozen gas—hydrogen, nitrogen, oxygen, carbon dioxide, and carbon monoxide—as well as water. Dust and pockets of unfrozen gas are mixed in, and everything is encased in a thick crust of frozen dust as dark as coal.

As the comet approaches the Sun, it begins to warm up. Near

the orbit of Jupiter, the Sun's heat is enough to turn its ices into gas, which leaks through cracks in the crust and surrounds the nucleus in a vast halo called the coma. As the comet plunges still closer to the Sun, this material spreads out behind it in the two enormous tails that make comets so spectacular. One is slightly curved and made of dust, which glows yellow-white as it reflects sunlight. The other tail—straight, often blue, and always pointing away from the Sun—is made of a thin scattering of gas pushed out millions of miles by the pressure of solar radiation.

HALLEY'S COMET

EDMUND HALLEY WAS THE FIRST PERSON TO REALIZE THAT COMETS ORBIT THE SUN AND SO ARE PERIODIC VISITORS TO OUR SKIES. HE ANALYZED THE ORBITS OF COMETS SEEN IN 1531, 1607, AND 1682, CONCLUDED THAT THEY WERE THE SAME OBJECT, AND PREDICTED THAT IT WOULD REAPPEAR IN 1758. SADLY, HALLEY DID NOT LIVE TO SEE THE REAPPEARANCE OF THE COMET THAT NOW BEARS HIS NAME (RIGHT), BECAUSE HE DIED IN 1742.

INSIDE A COMET

In deep space, a comet is an inert lump of dust and frozen gas. But as the comet approaches the Sun, the gas begins to boil off. It forms a thick "coma" that obscures the original lump, which now becomes the nucleus of the developing comet. Sometimes, the Sun heats pockets of gas trapped beneath the still-frozen surface. Eventually, they burst through, releasing jets of hazy debris that will form the comet's tails. Repeated passes of a comet around the Sun will in time rob it of anything that can still evaporate. Only a rocky core—if the comet has one—will remain, quietly orbiting the Sun as a tiny asteroid.

coma — exploding gas pockets

loose fragments — rocky core

HALLEY'S NUCLEUS

WHEN HALLEY'S COMET APPROACHED THE SUN IN 1986, THE SPACE PROBE *GIOTTO* FLEW THROUGH ITS COMA. SCIENTISTS WERE EXPECTING TO FIND THAT THE COMET WAS MADE OF MINERAL ELEMENTS SUCH AS IRON, CARBON, CALCIUM, AND SILICON. INSTEAD, *GIOTTO* FOUND HYDROGEN, NITROGEN, AND ORGANIC MOLECULES. THE NUCLEUS ITSELF WAS MAINLY ICE.

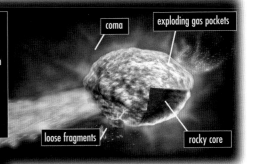

Hale-Bopp, one of the brightest comets of the twentieth century, was prominent in the night sky in the spring of 1997.

inert comet nucleus

ices begin to melt

Jupiter

tails die away

Sun

gas tail

fully formed comet

dust tail

LIFE OF A COMET

Far out in its orbit, the comet is nothing but a frozen nucleus. When it nears the orbit of Jupiter, it starts to thaw. Ice melts, and tails of gas and dust begin to form. As the comet continues inward to the Sun, the tails may expand to a spectacular length. They gradually die away after the comet swings around the Sun and heads off again to the cold fringes of the solar system.

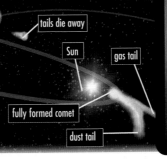

METEORS

Gaze upward on a clear night and sooner or later you will see streaks of light that race across the sky for up to a few seconds. Sometimes the streaks give off what look like sparks, or leave a glowing trail. You might even see a storm of streaks, all of which seem to radiate from a fixed point. The objects in question are meteors—natural fireworks displays that are put on by small particles of cometary debris called meteoroids as they fall through space and burn to a cinder high up in the Earth's

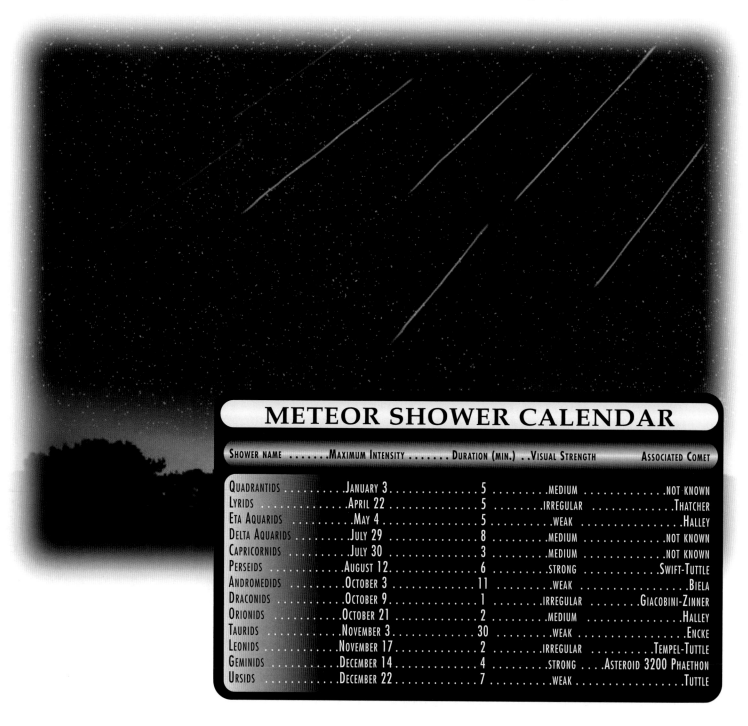

METEOR SHOWER CALENDAR

SHOWER NAME	MAXIMUM INTENSITY	DURATION (MIN.)	VISUAL STRENGTH	ASSOCIATED COMET
QUADRANTIDS	JANUARY 3	5	MEDIUM	NOT KNOWN
LYRIDS	APRIL 22	5	IRREGULAR	THATCHER
ETA AQUARIDS	MAY 4	5	WEAK	HALLEY
DELTA AQUARIDS	JULY 29	8	MEDIUM	NOT KNOWN
CAPRICORNIDS	JULY 30	3	MEDIUM	NOT KNOWN
PERSEIDS	AUGUST 12	6	STRONG	SWIFT-TUTTLE
ANDROMEDIDS	OCTOBER 3	11	WEAK	BIELA
DRACONIDS	OCTOBER 9	1	IRREGULAR	GIACOBINI-ZINNER
ORIONIDS	OCTOBER 21	2	MEDIUM	HALLEY
TAURIDS	NOVEMBER 3	30	WEAK	ENCKE
LEONIDS	NOVEMBER 17	2	IRREGULAR	TEMPEL-TUTTLE
GEMINIDS	DECEMBER 14	4	STRONG	ASTEROID 3200 PHAETHON
URSIDS	DECEMBER 22	7	WEAK	TUTTLE

SPACE TRAILS

To the ancients, the fiery trails of meteors must have looked very much as though a star had come adrift from the heavens and blazed its way across the sky. But the term "shooting star" for a meteor is misleading. Meteors are not stars, but the glowing tracks left by small particles called meteoroids that enter the Earth's atmosphere at high speed and burn up as they do so.

Meteoroids are particles of dust from comet tails that crossed our part of the solar system thousands of years ago. They orbit the Sun at speeds of many miles per second, and if they happen to encounter Earth's atmosphere, their speed increases from between 7 and 45 miles per second (11–72 kms).

At such speeds, the particles rapidly find themselves plunging through increasingly dense layers of the atmosphere. Although they weigh no more than a tiny fraction of an ounce, they carry more kinetic energy than a bullet from a gun. Within a fraction of a second, friction heat causes their outer layers to vaporize, throwing atoms into the atmosphere.

The atoms cause the surrounding air molecules to become ionized and they begin to glow brightly. The meteoroid itself soon breaks up, but not before it has left a trail of glowing air several yards wide and maybe 20 miles (32 km) long. On the ground, 50 miles (80 km) below,

anyone looking upward during the night hours will see this trail of destruction as the brief appearance of a shooting star.

Within seconds, the meteor is gone and the trail fades. Sometimes, however, the passage of the meteoroid releases so much energy that a train of glowing gas remains for several minutes.

SAME TIME

The Earth's part of the solar system is full of interplanetary debris that results in sporadic meteors. But far more interesting are the regular streams of meteoroids that give rise to meteor showers. These appear without fail on certain dates of the year when the Earth plows through a cloud of debris that has spread out in the wake of a comet's orbit probably within the past few hundred years.

From the ground, the meteors give the impression that they are radiating away from a particular point in the sky, known as the radiant. Simply the perspective, the view is like how parallel lanes of a highway seen from a bridge seem to radiate away from a single point on the horizon.

These meteor showers are named after the constellation in which the radiant appears. The Perseids, for example, regularly produce 60 to 100 meteors an hour around August 12, and appear to come from a point in Perseus. Some showers give rise to true meteor storms, in which hundreds of meteors appear.

WHAT IF?

...THE EARTH PASSED THROUGH A COMET'S TAIL?

Almost all of the regular meteor showers that happen at various times of the year take place when the Earth crosses the orbit of a comet and sweeps up the debris it leaves behind. Most of this debris tends to be scattered evenly around the comet's orbit. But some of the debris may be concentrated at one point in the orbit, and when the Earth crosses such a point, the resulting meteor shower can be spectacular. A good example is the Leonid shower, which revisits once every 33 years.

If the Earth were to pass through the actual tail of a comet, which contains still greater concentrations of debris (freshly swept off the comet by the effects of radiation from the Sun at close range), the result would be not a shower but a storm. Countless billions of cometary meteoroids would be swept up by the atmosphere, and the particles that create noticeable

meteor trails would be present in colossal numbers. Scientists can only speculate what kind of display this concentration of meteoroids would put on, but it would make the average fireworks display seem tame.

The chances of any of these cometary meteoroids reaching ground level would be very slim, so the storm, although dramatic, would not present any physical danger to the Earth's inhabitants. The danger would be if the Earth were hit by the comet's head—or even by just a part of it. The impact of separate fragments of comet Shoemaker-Levy 9 on Jupiter in 1994 clearly demonstrated the potential destructive power of a comet impact on a planet.

The Earth is thought to have been hit by just such a cometary fragment on June 30, 1908, when an object devastated some 850 square miles (2,200 square km) of forest in the Tunguska region of central Siberia in Russia.

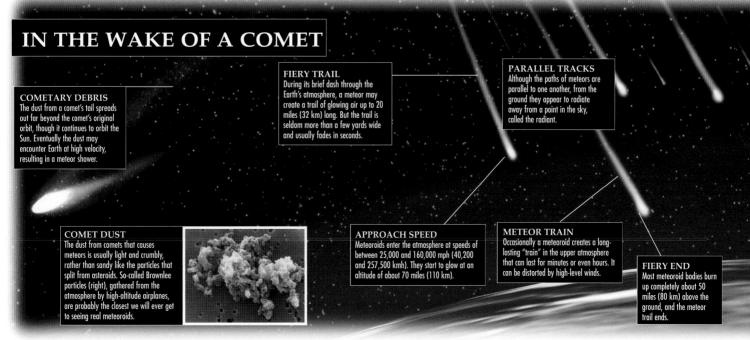

IN THE WAKE OF A COMET

COMETARY DEBRIS
The dust from a comet's tail spreads out far beyond the comet's original orbit, though it continues to orbit the Sun. Eventually the dust may encounter Earth at high velocity, resulting in a meteor shower.

FIERY TRAIL
During its brief dash through the Earth's atmosphere, a meteor may create a trail of glowing air up to 20 miles (32 km) long. But the trail is seldom more than a few yards wide and usually fades in seconds.

PARALLEL TRACKS
Although the paths of meteors are parallel to one another, from the ground they appear to radiate away from a point in the sky, called the radiant.

COMET DUST
The dust from comets that causes meteors is usually light and crumbly, rather than sandy like the particles that split from asteroids. So-called Brownlee particles (right), gathered from the atmosphere by high-altitude airplanes, are probably the closest we will ever get to seeing real meteoroids.

APPROACH SPEED
Meteoroids enter the atmosphere at speeds of between 25,000 and 160,000 mph (40,200 and 257,500 kmh). They start to glow at an altitude of about 70 miles (110 km).

METEOR TRAIN
Occasionally a meteoroid creates a long-lasting "train" in the upper atmosphere that can last for minutes or even hours. It can be distorted by high-level winds.

FIERY END
Most meteoroid bodies burn up completely about 50 miles (80 km) above the ground, and the meteor trail ends.

GLOSSARY

accretion A gradual process during which layers of a material are formed as small amounts are added over time.

asteroid A small, rocky celestial body found particularly between the orbits of Mars and Jupiter

barycenter The center of mass of two or more bodies, usually orbiting around each other, such as the Earth and the Moon.

centrifugal force In physics, a force that causes an object traveling in a circular path to move out and away from the center of its path.

chromosphere The region of the atmosphere of a star, like the Sun, located between the star's photosphere and corona.

coalesce To blend or grow together as one body.

comet An object traveling in outer space that develops a long, bright tail when it passes near the Sun.

condensation A process in which a gas cools and becomes a liquid.

contact The apparent touching or mutual tangency of any two celestial bodies or of the disk of one body with the shadow of another during an event like an eclipse.

convective zone The region of the Sun in which hot plasma rises, cools as it nears the surface, and falls to be heated and risen again.

corona The thin, outermost part of the atmosphere of a star, such as the Sun.

dwarf planet A celestial body that orbits the Sun and has a spherical shape but is not large enough to disturb other objects nearby.

ejecta Material thrown away, such as from a volcano.

ellipse An elongated circle.

gas giant One of the four outer planets in the solar system, consisting of Jupiter, Saturn, Uranus, and Neptune.

gibbous Relating to when the Moon or a planet is seen with more than half but not all its disk illuminated.

gravitational contraction The heat produced when a body, such as the Sun, shrinks under its own weight.

heavy bombardment phase A period of approximately eight hundred million years during which the early planets picked up material as they orbited the Sun.

helioseismology The study of vibrations in the material that makes up the Sun.

infrared Producing or using rays of light that cannot be seen and that are longer than rays that produce red light.

Kuiper Belt Object Any of the small icy bodies orbiting the Sun in the Kuiper Belt, generally having a diameter less than that of the dwarf planet Pluto.

light-year A unit of distance measuring the distance light travels in one year.

neap tide A tide of minimum range taking place during the first and third quarters of the Moon's cycle.

nuclear fusion A nuclear reaction in which nuclei combine to form much larger nuclei during which they release energy.

orbit To travel around something, such as a planet or the Moon, in a curved path.

penumbra A shaded region surrounding the dark central portion of a sunspot.

photosphere The luminous surface layer of the Sun or a star.

polar cleft A hole located above the North or South Pole of the Earth through which solar wind travels; part of the aurorae phenomenon.

protoplanet A hypothetical whirling gaseous mass within a giant cloud of gas and dust that rotates around the Sun and is believed to give rise to a planet.

protosun A gaseous cloud that undergoes gravitational collapse to form a sun.

radiation A kind of dangerous and powerful energy that is produced by radioactive substances and nuclear reactions.

retrograde rotation Describing when a body orbits backward.

satellite An object that moves around a larger planet, such as a moon.

solar nebula The hypothesized gaseous cloud from which the stars, planets, and Sun formed by condensation.

solar wind The continuous ejection of plasma from the Sun's surface into and through interplanetary space.

spectroscopy The study of spectra, especially experimental observation of optical spectra or mass spectra, to determine the properties of their source.

sunspot A dark spot that appears on the surface of the Sun.

terrestrial planet One of the four inner planets of the solar system, consisting of Mercury, Mars, Earth, and Venus; also called the rocky planets.

ultraviolet Describing a ray located beyond the visible spectrum at its violet end that has a wavelength shorter than those of visible light but longer than those of X-rays.

umbra The central dark part of a sunspot.

X-ray An electromagnetic radiation of an extremely short wavelength that is able to penetrate various thicknesses of solids and to act on photographic film as light does.

FURTHER INFORMATION

BOOKS

Bell, Jim. *The Space Book: From the Beginning to the End of Time, 250 Milestones in the History of Space & Astronomy.* New York: Sterling, 2013.

Berman, Bob. *The Sun's Heartbeat: And Other Stories from the Life of the Star That Powers Our Planet.* New York: Back Bay Books, 2012.

Chown, Marcus. *Solar System: A Visual Exploration of All the Planets, Moons and Other Heavenly Bodies That Orbit Our Sun.* New York: Black Dog and Leventhal, 2011.

Moltenbrey, Michael. *Dawn of Small Worlds: Dwarf Planets, Asteroids, Comets.* New York: Springer, 2016.

Wood, Charles A., and Maurice J.S. Collins. *21st Century Atlas of the Moon.* Morgantown, WV: University of West Virginia Press, 2012.

WEBSITES

NASA: Solar System Exploration
https://solarsystem.nasa.gov/planets
This comprehensive website includes detailed information on the eight planets in our solar system, as well as dwarf planets, comets, moons, and more. It also allows users to directly compare features of one planet against another.

NASA: Watch the Skies
www.nasa.gov/topics/solarsystem/features/watchtheskies/index.html
NASA's website provides up-to-date information and photographs of recent meteor showers, including pictures taken from the International Space Station.

Smithsonian National Air and Space Museum: Apollo to the Moon
http://airandspace.si.edu/exhibitions/apollo-to-the-moon/online/science
Read all about the Apollo Moon mission and the various experiments conducted by NASA astronauts to learn about our nearest neighbor.

Space.com: Earth's Sun: Facts About the Sun's Age, Size, and History
www.space.com/58-the-Sun-formation-facts-and-characteristics.html
This article provides information on the Sun's history and formation and includes a video about sunspots and how they form.

INDEX